AGAINST THE GRAIN

AGAINST THE GRAIN

BENTWOOD FURNITURE FROM THE COLLECTION OF FERN AND MANFRED STEINFELD

GHENETE ZELLEKE

EVA B. OTTILLINGER

NINA STRITZLER

THE ART INSTITUTE OF CHICAGO

This catalog accompanies the exhibition

AGAINST THE GRAIN

BENTWOOD FURNITURE FROM THE COLLECTION OF FERN AND MANFRED STEINFELD

curated by Ghenete Zelleke, on view at
The Art Institute of Chicago from June 5 to September 6, 1993.

Executive Director of Publications: Susan F. Rossen

Editor: David Krasnow

Production: Katherine Houck Fredrickson, assisted by Manine Rosa Golden

Photography of objects in the catalog by Sarah Wells, New York, except cat. nos. 42, 50, and 51, by Robert Hashimoto, Department of Imaging and Technical Services, The Art Institute of Chicago. Cat. no 7 and objects in the appendix are reproduced courtesy of Shelby Williams Industries, Inc.; appendix no. 37 by Sarah Wells.

The essay by Eva B. Ottillinger was translated from German by Matthew Heintzelmann.

Designed and typeset by Betty Binns Design
Three thousand copies were printed in duotone on eighty-pound Gleneagle Dull Enamel at Meridian Printing, East Greenwich, Rhode Island.

© 1993 The Art Institute of Chicago. All rights reserved. No portion of this publication may be reproduced in any manner whatsoever without prior written permission from the Publications Department of The Art Institute of Chicago.

DISTRIBUTED BY UNIVERSITY OF WASHINGTON PRESS

ISBN: 0-86559-113-X

LC: 93-111-94

CONTENTS

FOREWORD   6
JAMES N. WOOD
Director and President, The Art Institute of Chicago

PREFACE BY THE COLLECTOR   7
MANFRED STEINFELD

ACKNOWLEDGMENTS   8
GHENETE ZELLEKE
Associate Curator of European Decorative Arts and Sculpture, The Art Institute of Chicago

BENTWOOD FURNITURE IN CONTEXT: A STYLISTIC OVERVIEW   11
GHENETE ZELLEKE

BENTWOOD FURNITURE: A SUCCESS STORY   25
EVA B. OTTILLINGER
Wissenschaftlicher Mitarbeiter, Bundesmobiliensammlung, Vienna

CATALOG OF THE EXHIBITION   43
GHENETE ZELLEKE

THONET: MODERN FURNITURE SINCE 1922   101
NINA STRITZLER
Curator of Exhibitions, The Bard Graduate Center for Studies in the Decorative Arts

APPENDIX: OTHER FURNITURE FROM THE STEINFELD COLLECTION   113

CATALOG SOURCES   124

FOREWORD

One hundred forty years ago, the cabinetmaker and entrepreneur Michael Thonet established the firm Gebrüder Thonet, or Thonet Brothers. This company became one of the most innovative and successful enterprises in the history of furniture, manufacturing sturdy, lightweight, and inexpensive pieces that became classics of design. The exhibition and catalog *Against the Grain: Bentwood Furniture from the Collection of Fern and Manfred Steinfeld* celebrate the aesthetic and technical achievements of furniture constructed from bent wood. Although this process demands that rods of wood, made pliable by steam, be bent along the grain, we chose the title *Against the Grain* to suggest the revolutionary nature of the technique so successfully exploited by Michael Thonet, as well as the departure from contemporary norms his distinctive furniture effected. It was in bent wood that modernism was ushered into the interiors of the twentieth century.

In recent years, several books and exhibitions have given us substantial insights into the contributions of Thonet and some of its competitors. Most notable of these are *Bent Wood and Metal Furniture: 1850-1946* (1987), *Das Thonet Buch* (1987), and *Sitz-Gelegenheiten: Bugholz- und Stahlrohrmöbel von Thonet* (1989). In this catalog and the exhibition it accompanies, we have the opportunity to assess the important private collection of bentwood furniture assembled by Fern and Manfred Steinfeld in light of new documentation. During his tenure as chairman of Shelby Williams Industries, Mr. Steinfeld has acquired not only Thonet Industries (the successor to Gebrüder Thonet), but also a keen fascination with the lyrical forms and architectonic profiles of bentwood furniture. The Art Institute deeply appreciates Mr. and Mrs. Steinfeld's willingness to lend from their collection and their generous financial support of the exhibition and catalog. This is only the latest example of their contributions to this museum, which include the permanent endowment of a gallery and active participation on advisory committees.

As curator for this exhibition, Ghenete Zelleke of the Department of European Decorative Arts and Sculpture has shown commendable expertise in presenting the Steinfeld collection at the Art Institute in a cogent, scholarly, and visually interesting manner. Austrian bentwood furniture has long been a feature of American interiors, public and private. Gebrüder Thonet's first retail outlet in this country was opened in New York by 1873; the firm's work, and that of its competitor Jacob & Josef Kohn, was exhibited in 1876 at the Philadelphia Centennial Exposition. By the turn of the century, these firms also had outlets in Chicago and San Francisco. Chicago's emergence as a preeminent city for architecture roughly coincides with Thonet's development of the United States market, making our city an appropriate venue for an exhibition of the influential furniture it pioneered. The Art Institute's permanent collection is enriched by examples of industrially produced bentwood furniture by Thonet and Jacob & Josef Kohn, as well as by examples of traditionally crafted furniture by Austrian architects such as Josef Hoffmann. Interest in documenting contemporary Austrian work was at the core of the 1991 exhibition and catalog *Austrian Architecture and Design*. It is in this vein of exploration that we offer *Against the Grain: Bentwood Furniture from the Collection of Fern and Manfred Steinfeld*.

JAMES N. WOOD
Director and President
The Art Institute of Chicago

PREFACE BY THE COLLECTOR

My interest in bentwood furniture started in 1953, when I first visited the Great Northern Chair Company, a bentwood chair manufacturer on Chicago's near West Side that had been in operation since the early 1900s. The firm was recognized at that time as one of the leading United States makers of bentwood chairs for cafés, restaurants, nightclubs, hotels, and other institutions, and was surpassed only by the industry leader, Thonet Industries, Inc.

I was fascinated when I entered the bending room and saw steam coming out of retorts every time one of the workers removed a dowel or length of wood prior to bending. It was absolutely remarkable to see how pliable wood became under pressure of steam, and to see the final configurations that resulted from the bending process.

This company ceased operation early in 1954, and in a subsequent auction another investor and I became the owners of the chair facility. We immediately undertook a program to change the image and renamed the company Shelby Williams Manufacturing, Inc. We further embarked on a program of new designs, emulating Thonet Industries' popular bent plywood products and other styles reflecting the influence of Scandinavian design.

In 1987 Shelby Williams acquired Thonet Industries, Inc., from the Wickes Company, which included factories in York, Pennsylvania, and Statesville, North Carolina. The Statesville plant was still employing wood-bending principles originated by Michael Thonet in the 1850s. The Bentply facilities in York utilized high-frequency electronic machinery in bonding wood veneers to achieve intricate chair components. Along with Thonet Industries, Shelby Williams acquired a group of Thonet antiques, including one of Michael Thonet's early "Boppard" chairs. My interest in bentwood furniture accelerated and I started gathering examples of the most important pieces of bentwood furniture for my wife's and my private collection. Numerous pieces were purchased at auctions in New York and Europe, and others were acquired from collectors and galleries. To date, our collection comprises over two hundred representatives of every design era: Thonet's "classic" nineteenth-century period; the Viennese Secession; the Bauhaus; bent plywood; and Thonet today.

Though industry continues to create new products, the achievements of Gebrüder Thonet and Jacob & Josef Kohn will never be equalled. These Austrian firms produced technical marvels that astound the furniture maker of today. The principals of these companies possessed great manufacturing ingenuity and a keen sense of design. But they also introduced product development and marketing innovations unsurpassed in the twentieth century. This book is therefore dedicated not only to the craftsmen and designers whose work is discussed here in detail, but—equally important—to the owner-entrepreneurs who assumed the risk of bringing these new products to the marketplace. Their vision of design changes, coupled with a keen sense of consumer tastes and demands, made the chair the identifiable hallmark of every era from the Biedermeier period to today.

It is with great pleasure that Fern and I share our pride in their achievements with the people of Chicago and visitors to the Art Institute.

MANFRED STEINFELD

ACKNOWLEDGMENTS

I am deeply grateful to Fern and Manfred Steinfeld for making their collection of bentwood furniture available for exhibition at The Art Institute of Chicago, and for their generous financial underwriting of the exhibition and this catalog. Their passionate interest in the subject of bent wood and detailed knowledge of the field served as my constant inspiration and challenge.

This project has been enriched through the contributions of two colleagues who provided essays for the catalog. Eva B. Ottillinger brought her considerable knowledge of the histories of the Thonet, Kohn, and Mundus companies to bear on this project. Her involvement in a number of the most recent European catalogs and exhibitions devoted to bentwood furniture ensured that the latest scholarship has been incorporated into her essay. Dr. Ottillinger also kindly offered observations on many of the catalog entries. Nina Stritzler contributed a history of recent developments at the Thonet company and broadened our understanding of the evolution of twentieth-century furniture. A great debt is owed to Betty Binns, who designed this book, and to Sarah Wells, who photographed the bulk of the Steinfeld collection. Their sympathy for the lyrical and structural qualities of the furniture is obvious.

The staff of Shelby Williams Industries, Inc., both in Chicago and in Morristown, Tennessee, were generous with their time and cooperation. My thanks are due to Lorrayne Sloan and Paul Steinfeld in Chicago, and Robert Coulter, Ann Kramer, Duane Ware, Randy Hodges, Pete Barile and Frank Gray in Morristown.

Invaluable advice, assistance, documentation, and photographs were offered by many colleagues in this country and abroad: Christopher Wilk and Gareth Williams, The Victoria and Albert Museum, London; Christian Witt-Dörring and Ruperta Pichler, Österreichisches Museum für angewandte Kunst, Vienna; Alexander von Vegesack, Vitra Design Museum, Weil am Rhein; Lubomir Slavicek and Dagmar Sefcikova, National Gallery of Prague; Jaroslava Dobrincic, Prague and Rijeka; Klaus Thonet and Jutta Naumann, Gebrüder Thonet, Frankenberg; Simon Cobley, Orion Publishing Group Ltd., London; Bud Maclennan, Weidenfeld & Nicholson, London; Karen Zukowski and Joyce P. Kobasa, New York State Office of Parks, Recreation and Historic Preservation, Olana State Historic Site; Wayne Furman and Domenick Pilla, The New York Public Library; Suzelle Baudouin, Canadian Centre for Architecture, Montréal; Mariam Touba, The New-York Historical Society; Deborah Waters, Museum of the City of New York; Georg Kargl, Galerie Metropol, Vienna. Lisa Simpson's research for an exhibition of the Steinfeld collection at the Knoxville Museum of Art in 1990 was a useful starting point for my work. My thanks are also due to the translators of some of the German texts I consulted: Todd Bishop, Robert Hofmann, Paula Lee, Felix Tweraser, Inge Neumann, David Sgarlata, and Matthew Heintzelmann.

A catalog and exhibition are not possible without the participation of many museum staff—some of whom provide inspiration, and others who handle the many component tasks of such a project. Recognition must go to James N. Wood, Director and President of The Art Institute of Chicago, who conceived this exhibition and has given it his continued support. Ian Wardropper, Eloise W. Martin Curator of European Decorative Arts and Sculpture, and Classical Art, was steadfast in his support and generous with advice through all phases of this endeavor. Dorothy Schroeder, Assistant Director for Exhibitions and Budget, guided us through fiscal arrangements. This exhibition was coordinated with Christa C. Mayer Thurman, Curator and Conservator of Textiles, who installed a complementary group of Austrian and German textiles from the Art Institute's permanent collection. Susan Rossen, Executive Director of Publications, helped shape the catalog in its initial stages. David Krasnow, the editor for this project, has been a joy to work with. His attention to detail, sympathetic ear, and diplomatic skills coaxed the best from each author. Katherine Fredrickson oversaw the production of the catalog, coordinating the efforts of photographer, designer, and printer; she was ably assisted by Manine Golden. Robert Hashimoto of Imaging and Technical Services provided photographs of several pieces; Leslie Umberger took copystand photography. Barbara Hall and Suzanne Schnepp of the Conservation Department assembled condition reports for the loan objects, while Mary Mulhern of the Museum Registration Department coordinated their movements to and from the Art Institute. Reynold Bailey and his crew in Art Installation and Packing handled the collection within the museum. The installation was designed by Ann Wassmann and Donald DiSante of Graphic Services. Gallery work was coordinated through George Preston, Ronald Pushka, and John Bruyn in the Physical Plant Office, security through Robert Koverman. The resources of the Art Institute's Ryerson Library were vital in cataloging the Steinfeld collection: I wish in particular to thank Jack Brown for bringing unknown bentwood images to my attention, Alexis Petroff for patiently accommodating my large book requests, and Maureen Lasko, who was tireless in procuring what was not available in our stacks. Eloise W. Martin, Chairman of the Committee on European Decorative Arts and Sculpture, and Gloria Groom of the Department of European Painting each brought essential references to my attention. In the Department of European Decorative Arts and Sculpture, Marilyn Conrad, Kirsten Darnton, William Gross, Heidi O'Neill, and Steven Halvorsen contributed in many crucial ways to this exhibition and catalog and did so with patience, humor, and grace. Special recognition and my personal esteem go to Jessica Segal, an intern in our department during much of 1992, who was my constant resource in bringing this project to fruition.

GHENETE ZELLEKE
Associate Curator of European Decorative Arts and Sculpture
The Art Institute of Chicago

AGAINST THE GRAIN

MICHAEL THONET (CTR.) AND HIS SONS: MICHAEL (1824–1902), JOSEF (1830–1887), AUGUST (1829–1910), FRANZ (1820–1898), AND JAKOB (1841–1929).

BENTWOOD FURNITURE IN CONTEXT

A STYLISTIC OVERVIEW

GHENETE ZELLEKE

The enduring appeal of bentwood furniture is demonstrated by the pervasive use, even today, of models designed over one hundred years ago. This familiarity makes it difficult to see how the qualities that make bentwood so appealing—its light weight, durability, economical production, and ease of movement—were revolutionary in the early days of its production. The name Michael Thonet is synonymous with furniture made from bentwood elements. Under the direction of this German-born cabinetmaker, inventor, and entrepreneur, the Austrian firm Gebrüder Thonet introduced bentwood furniture to a wide public; along with later competitors such as Jacob & Josef Kohn, new methods of industrial production were developed.

This essay will review the stylistic, rather than technical, transformations of bentwood furniture in the period from Michael Thonet's first Biedermeier-inspired bentwood chair (cat. no. 2) to Kohn's successful marketing of modernist, architect-designed furniture in the period up to World War I (see, e.g., cat. no. 47). Three phases in bentwood furniture design during this time can be delineated. In the years up to the late 1870s, bentwood furniture was characterized by an unpretentious simplification of Biedermeier and Rococo revival aesthetics. In the second period, up to the turn of the century, bentwood furniture was consciously patterned on the revival-style furnishings of the time to attract the middle- and upper-class home market. From the beginning of the twentieth century, bent wood came under the direction of avant-garde architects and designers who infused the material with the aesthetic ideals of Viennese modernism. In production, these periods overlap one another, with the same designs produced, in some cases, for decades. The route by which bentwood furnishings gained acceptance—in aristocratic interiors, in public cafés and restaurants, and ultimately in private households—will be traced through contemporary images and a review of bent wood's critical reception.

From 1814 to 1815, Vienna was host to the Congress of Vienna, which presided over the reordering of the map of Europe. Monarchs who had fought to contain Napoleon's conquests were concerned to bring peace and stability to their borders and security to their thrones. Emperor Franz I of Austria (r. 1804–35), his successor Ferdinand (r. 1835–48), and Prince Klemens von Metternich, chancellor of Austria (1810–48), were intent on securing internal stability for the Austro-Hungarian Empire, and imposed on its people a repressive, authoritarian regime. Political participation was severely restricted. Censorship and the ever-present fear of informants curtailed vigorous public expression and suppressed dissent. With few public outlets for their energies, the population sought shelter in the home. Family virtues were exalted, and the arts that contributed to family comforts and pastimes were encouraged. Rooms in the bourgeois home were given over to a multitude of social, musical, literary, and other activities; a wide variety of furniture forms was created to satisfy each pursuit. The fixed position of furniture within a room was no longer the ideal, since pieces were moved around and reconfigured as the needs of the moment required.

Stylistically, the era from the Congress of Vienna to the political upheavals of 1848/49 is generally known as the Biedermeier period, though the years from the mid-1830s also saw the growth of historical revival styles that were to dominate the second half of the nineteenth century.[1] This period also coincided with the growth in numbers and affluence of the bourgeoisie, the principal market for the ever-expanding range of consumer goods made for the home.

The most prolific of furniture suppliers to the Viennese middle and upper classes during this period was Josef Ulrich Danhauser (1780–1829). In 1814 the Danhauser *Möbelfabrik* (furniture factory) was permitted to supply all manner of home furnishings hitherto restricted to specific guilds. Danhauser's enterprise was the largest of its time, supplying traditional cabinetwork, textiles for upholstery, wall coverings, glass, and metalwork. The variety of types of furniture in production and the possible variations for each item (see fig. 1) anticipate Michael Thonet's comprehensive inventory of furniture forms to fulfill every consumer need (see Ottillinger, fig. 9).

Michael Thonet's earliest pieces of furniture, produced in his native town of Boppard am Rhein, Prussia, from the late 1830s (see cat. no. 2), owe much to the curvilinear vocabulary of the Biedermeier style. The upholstered seat in combination with a wooden back, splayed legs, undulating back-and-leg profile, curved contour of the crest rail, and the use of finely figured wood veneers to mask the chair's construction and provide the principal decorative surface were all prefigured by Biedermeier examples. In the late 1850s, when Thonet moved in new technological directions by bending solid wood and dispensing with veneered surfaces (see cat. no. 7), the echoes of Danhauser's designs are still distantly heard (see fig. 1: "no. 18") in the double arch of the backrest, composed of two circular-sectioned rods of bent wood.

Thonet's early bentwood designs also reflected Viennese stylistic eclecticism, a manifestation of the nineteenth-century phenomenon of historicism, in which a wide range of styles from history were reworked, more or less accurately, in modern forms. The revival of the Gothic and Rococo had an impact on Viennese decorative arts and furnishings from around the 1830s. Thonet was involved in one of the major commissions in the Rococo revival style at the Liechtenstein Palace in Vienna. This city palace, built shortly after 1700, was remodeled over a ten-year period beginning in 1837 under the direction of the English architect Peter Hubert Desvignes (1804–1883). Thonet

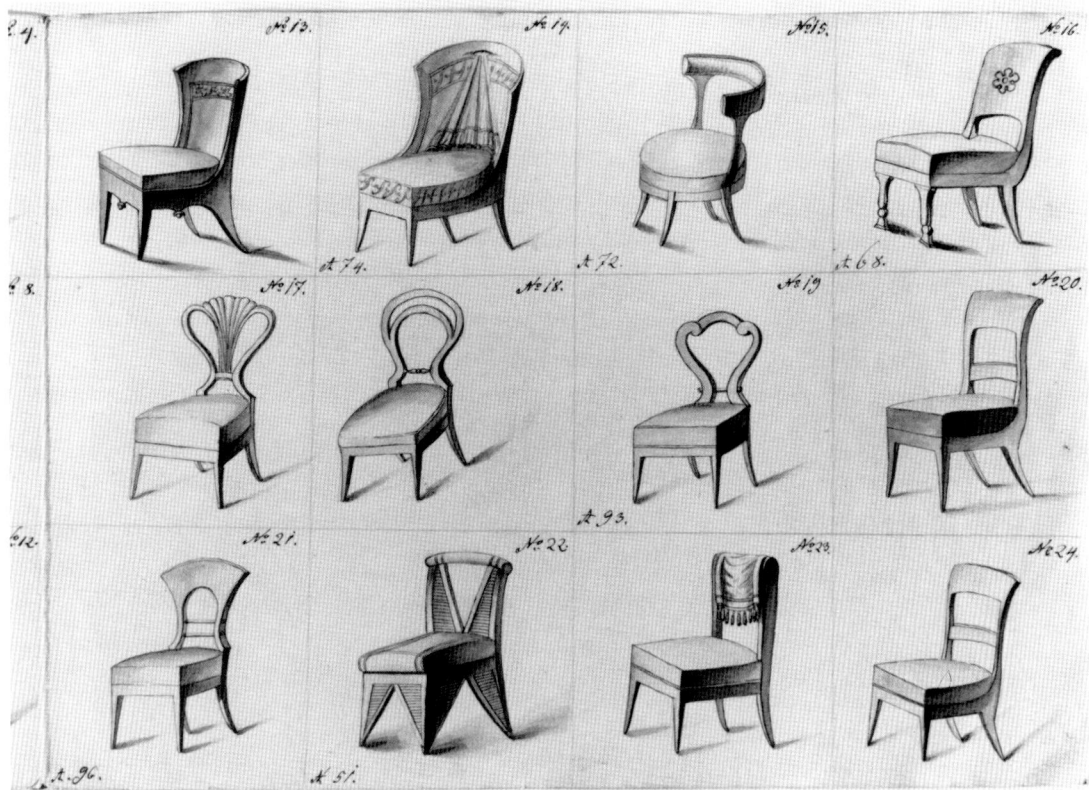

FIGURE 1
Design for chairs made by the Danhauser furniture factory, 1820/25
Courtesy Österreichisches Museum für angewandte Kunst

supplied parquet floors and chairs in the "second Rococo" manner for several of the principal palace rooms (see Ottillinger, fig. 1). In contrast to his work in the Biedermeier style, Thonet's chairs for Liechtenstein are characterized by arched backs, curved, almost cabriole, legs, and circular- (rather than rectangular-) sectioned rods. The influence of the Rococo revival continued in the bent laminate furniture Thonet sent to the world's first large international art and industrial products exhibition, held in London in 1851 (see cat. no. 4).

Thonet's first documented large commission was for a bentwood and caned side chair for the Café Daum in 1857, a fashionable coffeehouse frequented by the military in the vicinity of the imperial palace (see cat. no. 3). In the elaborate, double S-scroll inset for the back, Thonet continued to evoke the current taste for the Rococo revival in Viennese decorative arts.

Coffeehouses were essential to Viennese social, intellectual, and artistic life. The taste for drinking coffee had developed in the late seventeenth century, after Vienna withstood the Turkish siege of 1683. According to an imperial court commission's report to Empress Maria Theresa in 1747, the first public coffee sales were granted to four Greeks in 1700.[2] By 1714, regulations stipulated that no more than eleven public coffeehouse owners were permitted to operate in the city.[3] Their number grew, as did the importance of coffeehouses as forums for social life, discussion, political intrigue, gossip, and gambling:

> And just as tea, coffee, and chocolate have become all too popular throughout Europe, likewise one finds around thirty coffeehouses here, where they also sell cold mineral waters and liqueurs and where you can entertain yourself with billiards. In such places you generally meet writers, or those who busy themselves with newspapers or journals, discuss them, and talk about war and peace.[4]

The essence of Vienna's cafés was unchanged by the mid-nineteenth century.

With the commission for the Café Daum, the marriage was made between cafés and other public spaces and Thonet's uniquely portable, lightweight, and inexpensive bentwood chairs. They quickly became a ubiquitous feature of cafés and restaurants (see figs. 7, 8, and 10).

The novelty of bentwood chairs in the early years of Thonet's production is captured in an 1865 painting by Viktor Barvitius (fig. 2). Here, a single bentwood chair (Thonet's model number 8 or 14) is introduced into a bustling out-of-doors scene in which prosperous coffee drinkers are otherwise seated on more typically constructed occasional chairs.

In 1862 Gebrüder Thonet exhibited industrially manufactured bentwood furniture at London's International Exhibition, gaining a bronze medal and praise for its display: "they are not works of show but practical furniture for daily use—they are simple, graceful, light and strong."[5] Another view, articulated by the Viennese theoretician Jacob von Falke, one of the founders of the Österreichisches Museum für Kunst und Industrie, voiced reservations about the extent to which bent wood was appropriate in domestic interiors:

> Bentwood chairs, which are strong but light and are well-used in places like cafes, have no place in the home; they give us only a see-through silhouette, thin pieces of wood, when the eye really needs substantial objects full of form and color. They are also unimportant in their lack of colorful upholstery where the living room furniture must harmonize with the artistic effect of the room.[6]

Von Falke might have had an interior such as a Viennese drawing room of 1872 in mind (see fig. 3). Here, Thonet's model number 14 is informally disposed throughout the drawing room to supplement the heavily upholstered and trimmed armchairs and sofas arranged in conversation groups around tables. The Biedermeier period was the first to relax the symmetrical disposition of furniture against the walls. Furniture became mobile, to be rearranged about different "activity centers" within a single room.

The practical qualities of bentwood chairs were also appreciated in the United States, where the first Thonet office was opened in New York City by 1873. In 1875 the painter Frederic Edwin

FIGURE 2
Thursday in the Stromovka Park, 1865
Viktor Barvitius
Oil on canvas
Courtesy Národní Galerie v Praze (Prague)

FIGURE 3
A Viennese Drawing Room, 1872
Franz Alt
Watercolor
Photo: Charlotte Gere, *Nineteenth-Century Decoration: The Art of the Interior* **(London, 1989)**

Church purchased a set of chairs from Thonet Brothers for fifty-nine dollars for Olana, his recently built, Persian-inspired house in Hudson, New York.[7] Fifteen chairs of model number 17 survive at the house today. An 1884 photograph of Church's combination dining room and picture gallery shows three chairs arranged against the walls and a fourth, at the extreme right of the photograph, pulled up to the dining table (fig. 4). The draped circular table was routinely used for Church family meals and could be extended as required, with Thonet's chairs brought forward from the walls.

With their skeletal outline and lack of upholstery or carved ornament, these chairs almost fade into the background at Olana, in stark contrast to the other furnishings eclectically assembled from all over the world: an ornately carved and upholstered baroque-revival armchair, a Persian carpeted chest, a carved Italian cassone chest, and a small Middle Eastern table inlaid with ivory, tortoise shell, and mother-of-pearl. Like their European counterparts, middle- and upper-middle-class Americans appeared to be using bentwood furniture as occasional seating, adjuncts to the more heavily ornamented parlor furnishings that had clear status associations.

Upon the expiration in 1869 of Thonet's exclusive patent to manufacture bentwood furniture, other manufacturers began mass production to provide lightweight, easily assembled furniture. Jacob & Josef Kohn was only one of several bent wood firms in competition with Gebrüder Thonet, but by the beginning of this century it had become a serious contender for that part of the market most concerned with progressive furniture and modern designs. These two firms competed for the first time in Vienna in 1873 and three years later in 1876 at the Philadelphia Centennial Exposition. A critic of the exhibition commented on the strength and durability of bentwood furniture, observing that it was "especially adapted to use in summer-houses, where its lightness and coolness make it agreeable to the eye and touch."[8] Green houses and conservatories were considered suited to furnishing with bent wood, as a turn-of-the-century drawing shows (fig. 5). Amid the tiled and

FIGURE 4
Dining room and picture gallery at Olana, 1884
Courtesy of New York State Office of Parks, Recreation and Historic Preservation, Olana State Historic Site

FIGURE 5
Jardin d'hiver (Vue d'ensemble en perspective), c. 1900
Photo: Georges Rémon, *Intérieurs Modernes*, pl. 28 (Paris: Librarie de l'Art Ancien et Moderne [1900])

trellised walls of a French conservatory or "winter garden" filled with wicker furniture, one sees a single bentwood rocker resembling Gebrüder Thonet's model number 10 (see cat. no. 15).

Examples of both Thonet's and Kohn's furniture at the 1876 exhibition were illustrated in *Harper's Weekly* (see fig. 6). In describing their exhibits, Harper's critic noted:

> Messrs. Thonet Brothers and Messrs. Jacob & Joseph [sic] Kohn, of Vienna, make very handsome displays of elegant bent-wood furniture…which first came into use about thirty years ago. The frames are of beech wood, painted black and highly polished, with the exception of the frame-work of the aquarium and flower stand in the centre, which is striped with gold.[9]

It is apparent from the illustration that a new, more elaborate style for bentwood furniture was being introduced by the two rivals. Critics such as von Falke, who had pointed to the unsuitability of bent wood for the living room of the time, were presented with bentwood furniture that could be purchased caned or upholstered, with elaborately carved elements such as the swans and stylized dolphins on the stand and rocking chair, to better serve the taste for highly decorated furniture.

Two of the more elaborate pieces illustrated, the "aquarium and flower stand" and the heavily upholstered rocking chair, may be attributed to Kohn, as almost identical pieces are illustrated in its twenty-seven-page American catalog of about 1881.[10] Both Kohn and Thonet produced the side chair (Thonet's model number 16), but the thickly padded "rocking sofa" is a model by Thonet. Kohn, in looking for a niche in the market to compete with the entrenched Thonet, made a determined effort to produce bentwood furniture for formal drawing rooms, in addition to competing in the market that Thonet had so successfully established—the public spaces of cafés and restaurants, and secondary rooms of private homes. At the 1878 Paris Exposition Universelle, Kohn again responded to public taste for ornate types of furniture, proclaiming:

> Furniture has just been produced featuring sculpted ornaments, carvings, and inlay, in such a way that great elegance and perfection of style complement the excellent qualities for which this furniture has been well-regarded—durability, economy, and utility.[11]

In the last two decades of the nineteenth century, Kohn, Thonet, and other manufacturers echoed the taste for historicist furnishings, offering Gothic- and Renaissance-revival furniture in bent wood with elaborately carved crest rails, turned or carved legs, and tufted and fringed upholstery to appeal to the shifting fashions in interiors and the consumer's wish for stylish display. Their

FIGURE 6

Bentwood furniture exhibited at the Philadelphia Centennial Exposition, 1876

Photo: *Harper's Weekly*, October 28, 1876, p. 876; courtesy of the General Research Division, The New York Public Library, Astor, Lenox and Tilden Foundations

established market, the public cafés, theaters, and cabarets, nevertheless remained an important staple and support for the bentwood market throughout Europe and the rest of the world, (see fig. 7). These extensive offerings were most fully displayed in Gebrüder Thonet's 120-page catalog of 1895.

Just over forty years after Michael Thonet furnished the Café Daum with his recently designed chairs, another Viennese café was to play a pivotal role in bentwood furniture design. In 1899, the architect Adolf Loos introduced a red-stained bentwood chair manufactured by Jacob & Josef Kohn into the Café Museum (cat. no. 45; see fig. 8). This marked the beginning of a new era for bent wood in which anonymous furniture designers working for the manufacturers were displaced by high-profile architects and independent designers.

Loos was an ardent Anglophile and also an admirer of America, having spent time in both London and Chicago.[12] He was especially critical of the nostalgia for the past which had such an impact on the historicist styles of the second part of the nineteenth century. Loos bitingly parodied backward-looking, late nineteenth-century Austria, whose students might exclaim:

> Oh, how lovely it was in the Middle Ages! And especially in the Renaissance!... And now? Simply gruesome.... We want to stand fast like rocks in the midst of the ugly bustle of modern life.... Down with the telephone! But if it must be? Then we want to arrive at a compromise. We will provide the telephone booths with Rococo ornament and the telephone receivers with Rococo handles. Or Gothic. Or Baroque. Any way the customer wishes it.[13]

FIGURE 7
At the Moulin Rouge, 1892
Henri de Toulouse-Lautrec
Oil on canvas
The Art Institute of Chicago, Helen Birch Bartlett Memorial Collection, 1928.610

FIGURE 8
Café Museum, 1899
Courtesy Archiv Gebrüder Thonet GmbH, Frankenberg

In the same essay, Loos praised the English system by which the best work of art-school students was regularly taken up by manufacturers for production so that "Art and life complement one another harmoniously. But with us the saying goes: art versus life!"[14] Loos's views on the benefits to be derived from linking trained designers with industry were reflected in practice at Kohn. In the same year that the Café Museum was opened, Kohn became the first of the bent wood companies to hire a design director in the person of Gustav Siegel (1880–1970), a young architecture student and trained cabinetmaker. It was a turning point for Kohn and for furniture design.

In 1897, the painter Gustav Klimt spearheaded the formation of a new exhibition society known as the Secession. Under his direction, a group of artistic rebels, including Otto Wagner (1841–1918), Josef Hoffmann (1870–1956) and Koloman Moser (1868–1918), reacted against the academic and tradition-bound aspirations of the conservative art establishment, the hierarchical division between the fine and applied arts, and the stylistic crutch of historicism. They sought to breathe a new and contemporary spirit into artistic life, crafts, and industry in Vienna. The group's motto, "To the age its art, to art its freedom" (inscribed on the exterior of the Secession building, across the street from the Café Museum), captured the ambitions of the group to break with the traditions of the past and formulate a modern artistic vocabulary for the coming century. The importance of the Café Museum in the life of the aesthetic avant-garde is captured in this reminiscence of Josef Lux:

> Every day we sat across from the Secession in the intimate circle of the "black coffee corner" of Café Museum, where it was a sign of distinction to belong to the regulars' table, whose visitors included, besides [Otto] Wagner, the founders of the Wiener Werkstätte, and Gustav Klimt, the artistic genius of the time.... For five years, until my departure from my Viennese homeland in 1906, I would come every day after dinner to the eventful "black coffee hour," where we tore down the world and built it anew.... Whatever was important in European art of the time made an appearance in Vienna, in the Secession and at our table.[15]

The proximity of the Secession building to the Café Museum undoubtedly gave the progressive artists and architects who frequented the café insights into the potentials of bent wood that were to influence their work in succeeding years.

Through exhibitions organized by the Secession from 1898 on, contemporary European art was introduced to Vienna through shows in which fine and decorative arts were integrated as equal partners within coordinated environments. This concept of the interior as a *Gesamtkunstwerk*, a "total work of art," under the direction of a single designer influenced the progressive lines of bentwood furniture in the years up to World War I.

The reinvigorated Viennese artistic environment, as well as European developments of Art Nouveau, were prominently displayed in Paris at the Exposition Universelle of 1900. Interesting parallels can be drawn between the installations of the Secessionists, in particular that of Josef Hoffmann, and those of the commercial bent wood manufacturers, especially Jacob & Josef Kohn. Hoffmann designed the room display of the School of Applied Arts in which the borders of the walls were stenciled with elongated and swirling patterns of lines (see fig. 9).

Kohn's installations, which included bentwood furnishings and room dividers by the newly hired Gustav Siegel, won the grand prize (see Ottillinger, fig. 11). Siegel's room partitions in particular show the influence of Art Nouveau, echoing Hoffmann's stenciled interior. Siegel manipulated parallel ribs of bent wood just as Hoffmann drew multiple strands of color around the edges and into the corners of the School of Applied Arts installation. Kohn's innovative use of bent wood, its special sympathy with the modern aesthetic, was favorably remarked upon by Austrian critics, to Thonet's detriment:

FIGURE 9

School of Applied Arts (Vienna) exhibit at the Exposition Universelle, Paris, designed by Josef Hoffmann

Photo: *The Paris Exhibition 1900*, p. 309, Courtesy Collection Centre Canadien d'Architecture/Canadian Centre for Architecture, Montréal

> The Viennese specialty of manufacturing bentwood furniture accommodated itself well into the designs of the modern style and presented itself so preeminently. Indeed, the products which Thonet exhibited leave much to be desired, so much more refined and tasteful are the dining room and particularly the bedroom of the company J. & J. Kohn; the table, bed, chest, and chaise longue are, in their design and color, simple, tasteful, and practical.[16]

Austrian bent wood was remarkably resistant to the seductions of French and Belgian Art Nouveau, exemplified by designers such as Eugène Gaillard, Edward Colonna, and Georges de Feure, each of whom was featured at the Paris exhibition of 1900. Gebrüder Thonet's catalog of 1904 offered only two designs that truly reflected this style: an arm- and side chair en suite with a settee, model number 13, and a two-tiered stand (cat. no. 42). This is somewhat surprising considering the ease with which bent wood could be manipulated through almost any curve. But the Austrian industry was to embark on a new, and particularly Viennese direction, along the lines already laid out by Kohn at the Paris exhibition.

Siegel's continued importance at Kohn was remarked upon in *The Studio Year Book* of 1908:

> Gustav Siegel…is devoting all his energy to the solving of the bent-wood problem, ably supported by Messrs. J. & J. Kohn. The development during the past year in this special branch of art justifies predicting a great future. The designs are a great advance on previous ones, and prove the advantage of having a good artist on the spot.[17]

But Siegel was only one of a number of designers responsible for revitalizing Kohn's bentwood furniture. Josef Hoffmann, who was responsible for many of the Secession's installations since 1898, applied his reductivist, geometric designs to bent wood while advocating a return to handcrafts within a multidisciplinary workshop. In 1903, Hoffmann and Koloman Moser established a craft studio known as the Wiener Werkstätte (Vienna Workshop). In their "Work Program" of 1905, they outlined the reasons behind its foundation:

> The boundless evil, caused by shoddy mass-produced goods and by the uncritical imitation of earlier styles, is like a tidal wave sweeping across the world….The machine has largely replaced the hand and the businessman has supplanted the craftsman….We wish to create an inner relationship linking public, designer and worker and we want to produce good and simple articles of everyday use. Our guiding principle is function, utility our first condition, and our strength must lie in good proportions and proper treatment of material.[18]

Influenced by the theoretical goals of the English Arts and Crafts movement, the Werkstätte promoted hand craftsmanship while also, rather hesitantly, admitting the utility of machine production:

> We should also like to draw attention to the fact that we too are aware that, under certain circumstances, an acceptable article can be made by mechanical means, provided that it bears the stamp of manufacture, but it is not our purpose to pursue that aspect yet.[19]

Hoffmann's use of bent wood technology allowed the most progressive designs to be marketed to a wider audience than the elite for whom he designed private homes full of handcrafted furniture. Though the Werkstätte eschewed industrial processes within the workshop, Hoffmann actively incorporated furniture made with bent wood technology into his exhibition installations and in one of the Werkstätte's earliest commissions, the building and furnishing of the Purkersdorf Sanatorium, an elegant spa outside Vienna. Hoffmann designed a side chair (cat. no. 50) first produced by Kohn for the dining room of the Sanatorium around 1904 and subsequently marketed to the public as part of a matching suite. It clearly shows a new emphasis on geometry

FIGURE 10
Cabaret Fledermaus, interior designed by Josef Hoffmann, c. 1907
Photo: *Deutsche Kunst und Dekoration,* December 1908, p. 158

FIGURE 11
Kunstschau entrance hall, designed by Josef Hoffmann, 1908
Photo: *The Studio Year Book of Decorative Art,* 1910, p. 223

that informs both the decorative and structural components of this chair: the spheres under the seat have replaced the circular leg ring of the nineteenth century in providing stability, and two columns of circles piercing the back splat lend decorative interest.

The early twentieth-century café continued to be an important market for bentwood chairs (see fig. 10). The same vocabulary of ornament found in Hoffmann's chair for the Sanatorium is seen in the chair he designed around 1906 for the Cabaret Fledermaus (cat. no. 57). Hoffmann completely integrated the interior, creating a *Gesamtkunstwerk* in black and white. In 1905 Klimt, Hoffmann, and others quit the Secession, eventually to stage an independent exhibition known as the Kunstschau (Art Show) in 1908. A "small country house" fully furnished with Kohn's bentwood furniture was among the several exhibition buildings Hoffmann designed. A reclining armchair (cat. no. 53), a hybrid of a nineteenth-century English form and the Purkersdorf side chair, was featured in one of its rooms (see fig. 11). The careful integration of the interior as seen in the Cabaret Fledermaus was achieved in this room through the studied choices of upholstery and patterns for the floor.

A 1906 Kohn advertisement proclaimed the range of applications for their furniture:

> "Furnishing of entire houses in modern style after designs by eminent artists. Bentwood furniture for hotels, restaurants and for every other purpose...Application of art and craft to the bentwood furniture industry."[20]

In its catalog of the same year, Kohn carefully separated the more traditional lines of bentwood furniture designed in the nineteenth century from those of recent design that were described as *Meubles de salon, style moderne*. These new designs by or after Siegel and Hoffmann were marketed by Kohn for the private home. In contrast, Hoffmann was using bent wood when large numbers of movable chairs were required, as in the Purkersdorf Sanatorium, or in his exhibition installations. Most of the furnishings for his private commissions were handcrafted, labor-intensive, and costly.[21]

Kohn was so well associated with avant-garde design that a 1916 catalog, printed two years after the firm's merger with the bent wood conglomerate Mundus, was published under the name Kohn alone. Thonet was slow to respond to the interest in architect-designed furniture; it was not until 1905 that Marcel Kammerer (1878–1969), Otto Wagner's associate, joined Thonet. Work influenced by Viennese architects' designs first appeared in the firm's catalog supplements of 1905 and 1907 and in advertising photographs of Thonet's showroom interiors (see fig. 12), in which updated forms, such as a tall-case clock, were introduced (see cat. no. 61).

The Werkstätte's emphasis on the principles of function, utility, and "proper treatment of material" can be seen to have broadly informed bentwood furniture production between 1900 and 1914. As with Gebrüder Thonet's models of the first few decades after its establishment in 1853, bent wood was ideally suited to the contexts in which it appeared: as exhibition furniture as well as situations in which large numbers of chairs were required, as in the Purkersdorf Sanatorium and the Cabaret Fledermaus. It is ironic that much of the furniture designed from 1900 to World War I by contemporary architects, designed specifically to address contemporary aesthetic concerns and often keyed to particular interiors, remains very much of its time, reflecting notions of modernism current for less than two decades. Many of the early twentieth-century Viennese interiors stressed the subordination of individual element to the whole. When pieces are taken out of context, they retain their striking individuality. The very absence of such a didactic program in nineteenth-century bent wood production and the fact, as von Falke expressed it, of the furniture's transparency make those

FIGURE 12
Display of Thonet furniture "in the modern style," sales catalog of 1907/08
Courtesy Archiv Gebrüder Thonet GmbH, Frankenberg

earlier mass-production examples appear timeless. Today it is the more anonymously designed objects of the nineteenth century, such as Thonet's chair models 4 and 14 (cat. nos. 3, 7)—created without a particular location in mind, and without an overwhelming aesthetic—that transcend the styles of their time, and continue to blend easily into late twentieth-century interiors.

NOTES

1. The term Biedermeier, a conjunction of the common German surname Meier and *bieder*, meaning plain, first appeared in 1853 as the surname of a poet invented by Germans Adolph Kussmaul and Ludwig Eichrodt. Under this name they published poems that satirized the unpretentious and homebound virtues of the plain Austrian man. As a term denoting a particular style, Biedermeier came into use in the 1890s. For a detailed discussion of the evolution of the term and the characteristics of the period, see Georg Himmelheber, *Biedermeier Furniture,* trans. and ed. by Simon Jervis (London, 1974), pp. 23–28; and *Vienna in the Age of Schubert: The Biedermeier Interior, 1815–1848*, exh. cat. Victoria and Albert Museum, London (1979).

2. Cited in Christian Brandstätter, *Das Wiener Kaffeehaus* (Vienna, 1978), p. 40.

3. Ibid., p. 41, citing "Coffeehouse-owner's license of Charles VI," 1714.

4. Ibid., citing J. B. Küchelbecker, 1730. Felix W. Tweraser of the University of Chicago provided translations from Brandstätter.

5. Jury report on Thonet's display at the 1862 International Exhibition in London, cited by Ole Bang, "Thonet and England," *The Journal of the Decorative Arts Society, 1850 to the Present,* no. 11 (1987), p. 31.

6. Jacob von Falke, *Die Kunst im Haus* (1871), as cited by Eva B. Ottillinger, "Thonet als Vorbild—Vorbilder für Thonet: Das Bugholztechniken und die Zeitgenossen," in *Sitz-Gelegenheiten: Bugholz- und Stahlrohrmöbel von*

Thonet, exh. cat. Germanisches Nationalmuseum, Nürnberg (1989), p. 57. Translation kindly provided by Todd Bishop, Harvard University.

7. The canceled check for the purchase, dated June 23, 1875, is in the archive of the Olana State Historic Site. I am most grateful to Karen Zukowski, Curator of the Olana State Historic Site, for bringing this to my attention and for sharing with me the "Dining Room/Gallery Furnishings Plan" in the unpublished manuscript "Olana Furnishings Plan" by Karen Zukowski et al. I am grateful too to Christa C. Mayer Thurman, Curator and Conservator of Textiles at The Art Institute of Chicago, for first bringing the suite of bentwood furniture at Olana to my attention. For a full discussion of the Hudson River home, see James Anthony Ryan, "Frederic Church's Olana: Architecture and Landscape as Art," in *Frederic Edwin Church,* exh. cat. National Gallery of Art, Washington, D.C. (1989), pp. 126–56.

8. Walter Smith, *The Masterpieces of the Centennial International Exhibition,* vol. II (Philadelphia, [1876]), p. 422.

9. *Harper's Weekly* (October 28, 1876), p. 870. I wish to thank Wayne Furman, Office of Special Collections, and Domenick Pilla, Technical Assistant for Copy Services, at the New York Public Library for locating this reference.

10. A copy of Kohn's catalog, entitled *Manufactories of Massive Bent Wood Furniture of Jacob & Josef Kohn,* is among the trade catalogs at Winterthur Library. The title page records the awards received by Kohn to date: at Philadelphia, 1876; Diplôm d'Honneur, Anvers, 1879; first prize with special mention, Sydney, 1879; Niederösterreichische Gewerbeausstellung, Ehren-Diplom, 1880; first prize, Melbourne, 1881.

11. International Exhibition, Paris 1878: *Catalogue of the Austrian Section,* vol. 3 (Vienna, n.d.), p. 86, cited in Christian Witt-Dörring, "Bent Wood Production and the Viennese Avant-garde: The Thonet and Kohn Firms, 1899–1914," in Derek E. Ostergard, ed., *Bent Wood and Metal Furniture: 1850–1946,* exh. cat. American Federation of Arts, New York (1987), p. 96.

12. The appeal of America for Loos was in what he saw as its extreme practicality and lack of history: "Art is the Romanticism of primitive peoples. Cultural development is, as America proves, ridding one's self of art and becoming practical." Remark attributed to Loos by Emil Szittya, 1923, as cited in Brandstätter (note 2), p. 90. My thanks to Felix W. Tweraser and Inge Neumann for kindly translating several passages dealing with the Café Museum.

13. Adolf Loos, "English Schools in the Austrian Museum," *Die Wage* (January 29, 1898), trans. in Adolf Loos, *Spoken into the Void: Collected Essays, 1897–1900* (Cambridge, Mass., 1982), p. 107.

14. Ibid., p. 109.

15. Cited in Brandstätter (note 2), p. 86.

16. Ludwig Abels, "Wiener Tischlerarbeit auf der Parisen Weltausstellung," *Das Interieur,* vol. I (1900), p. 134. Todd Bishop kindly provided this translation.

17. *The Studio Year-Book of Decorative Art* (London, 1908), p. xlvi.

18. Josef Hoffmann and Koloman Moser, "The Work-Programme of the Wiener Werkstätte" (1905), repr. in Tim Benton, Charlotte Benton, and Dennis Sharp, eds, *Architecture and Design 1890–1939* (New York, 1975), pp. 36–37.

19. Ibid., p. 37.

20. Kohn advertisement reproduced in Stefan Asenbaum and Julius Hummel, eds., *Gebogenes Holz: Konstruktive Entwürfe Wien 1840–1910,* exh. cat. Kunstlerhaus Wien, Vienna (1979).

21. Ottillinger (note 6), p. 61.

BENTWOOD FURNITURE PRODUCTION

A SUCCESS STORY

EVA B. OTTILLINGER

The development of bentwood furniture production from Michael Thonet's cabinetmaking workshop at Boppard into a major international industry is a classic example of the mechanisms of the industrial revolution. The success of bent wood lay not only in a forward-looking invention, but also in a flexible application of the technology, in the selection of production sites, in the constant expansion of the product lines offered, and not least of all in marketing tactics. Three centers of production (Boppard am Rhein, Vienna, and Moravia) correspond to three stages in the evolution of wood-bending techniques (using laminated strips, laminated rods, and solid wood). In each case, this parallel progression was brought about by the appearance of major competitors. The subject of this essay is the fascinating and complex interrelationship between technical development and the history of the Thonet company, on the one hand, and economic conditions and competition, on the other.[1]

THE WORKSHOP AT BOPPARD (1819–42)

The master cabinetmaker Michael Thonet (1796–1871) established his furniture carpentry workshop in 1819 in Boppard am Rhein, near the workshop of the famed Neoclassical furniture maker David Roentgen at Neuwied. Around 1835 Thonet began to experiment with bending wood for chair parts, studying the layered gluing technique called lamination, which had been employed in the late eighteenth century by Thomas Chippendale and Jean Joseph Chapuis, among others, as well as in the Windsor chair.[2] He cut sheets of wood veneer (in the direction of the grain) into strips, boiled them in glue, and pressed bundles of the veneers into the desired shapes with the aid of curved molds. His innovative use of this technique could hardly be distinguished visually from contemporary chairs made out of cut and joined solid pieces of wood and covered by veneer. Thonet used lamination to produce the type of side chair fashionable at that time, along with matching armchairs and benches, in small series (cat. no. 2). He no longer produced by commission from a client, but rather kept a store of his models on hand, thus taking an important step in the industrialization of furniture production. Thonet's chairs were considerably lighter and could be produced with less material, much more cheaply and quickly, than those of customary cabinetmakers.

On July 5, 1841, Michael Thonet and his investor Johann Walter van Meerten, a businessman from Boppard, applied for a patent on his technique in Paris, which was granted on November 16 for a period of fifteen years—although a year before in Prussia his request had been denied due to "lack of innovation." Thonet undertook the high costs of the patent procedure not so much to protect this technique for his own production, but so he could offset his large debt by selling licenses for the technique to other producers. He was unable to realize this plan, however. Lacking sufficient clientele in Boppard, Thonet took his wares to a Koblenz trade show in August 1841, where the Austrian chancellor, Prince Klemens von Metternich (himself from the Rhineland) was so impressed by the display that he invited Thonet to test his technique in Vienna, the metropolis of the Habsburg monarchy. This was an attractive offer, for the imperial capital—with its court, palaces of the nobility, and wealthy bourgeoisie—offered opportunities on a scale completely different from that of Boppard, a small town on the Rhine.

Thonet's first German competitors also appeared at this time. The furniture manufacturer Philipp J. Kertell of Bingen participated with Thonet in the General German Industrial Exposition in 1842 in Mainz.[3] For six to eight florins, Kertell offered "several chairs and seats built with side pieces bent in a unique fashion…of pleasant lightness combined with a rare sturdiness."[4] This seems to have involved a technique similar to Thonet's, but we have not found a clue to the actual physical appearance of the models. Another competitor was Peter Mündnig or Mündnich, a court cabinetmaker from Koblenz who exhibited at the General German Trade Exposition in 1844 in Berlin "a chair in separate pieces, glued together from several pieces of walnut which…promises a great durability despite its delicacy and lightness, but which, in the case of eventual breakage, would be very difficult to put back together."[5] In the Victoria and Albert Museum in London, a bentwood chair identified as from Mündnich of Koblenz perfectly matches the early Boppard models of Michael Thonet in its formation, and indeed was thought to be by Thonet when acquired.

Thonet's decision to move to Vienna in 1842 was motivated not only by his oppressive credit burden—his workshop, with a store of eight hundred models, was about to be seized, and a shipment intended for the Viennese court was confiscated in Frankfurt—but also by the pressure of competition that had arisen in the Rhineland despite the patent that protected his method.

THE BEGINNINGS IN VIENNA (1842–49)

Michael Thonet confronted an entrenched guild structure when he arrived in Vienna in 1842. Until freedom of trade was established in 1859, only "citizen masters" were allowed to practice a trade. An exception was the so-called factory authorization, used for example by Josef Ulrich Danhauser's "Establishment for All Types of Furniture," the most important Viennese furnishing enterprise in the Biedermeier period. This authorization entitled Danhauser to offer all necessary parts for furnishing—furniture, room textiles, mirrors, lamps, etc.—without being exposed to the charge of "trade interference."

As imperial capital and residence, Vienna was a recognized center of furniture carpentry in the first half of the nineteenth century. Its craftsmen were praised above all for the quality of their "curved wares"—those light, richly curved Biedermeier pieces made out of veneered whole wood.[6] In the 1840s, Vienna boasted more than 1,500 master cabinetmakers and more than 150 upholstering businesses;[7] when Michael Thonet arrived in Vienna, there was no urgent demand for immigrant entrepreneurs in his trade.

On July 6, 1842, Thonet and van Meerten presented his products with the request for a recommendation before the Lower Austrian Trade Association, a group of craftsmen and industrialists that had assigned itself the task of promoting domestic trade through information on technical innovations and recent formal developments. Because Thonet was not ready to present details of his production technique—though he referred to a patent application already underway—the commission did not see fit to draw up a recommendation.[8] But he had succeeded in informing his Viennese audience of his technique, and by July 16, 1842, he received the patent "to bend any type of wood, even the most brittle, into the desired forms and curves by chemical and mechanical means." The prerequisites were in place to begin production according to this privilege; because of his bankruptcy in Boppard, however, Thonet lacked the necessary means to build an independent business in Vienna. He moved his family to Vienna anyway and started producing "inexpensive chairs" with his sons in the "Royal-Imperial Patent Woodbronze and Furniture Factory" of Clemens List in Mariahilf,[9] which, with one hundred workers, was one of the largest furniture makers in Vienna. As three examples recently discovered in the Viennese art trade illustrate,[10] these were simplified variations on the Boppard type, in which the bent parts were limited to the backrest frames and parts of the side frame.

FIGURE 1

Side chair for the Palais Liechtenstein, Vienna, 1843/49 (left and right)

Designed and produced by Michael Thonet

Wood laminate

Courtesy Archiv Gebrüder Thonet GmbH, Frankenberg (Photo: L. Chmel)

However, the aged List soon retired, and advised Thonet to contact the English architect Peter Hubert Desvignes, who since 1837 had been engaged in expanding and refurnishing the Baroque city palace of Prince Alois Josef I of Liechtenstein in the opulent forms of the Rococo revival *(zweites Rokoko)*.[11] Desvignes obviously recognized the forward-looking possibilities of Thonet's process and offered to Thonet that he work independently within the workshop of the Viennese cabinetmaker and parquet-maker Carl Leistler (1805–1857), who had the contract for the expensive furniture and parquet floors. Thonet executed the intricately pieced parquet floors with the aid of his bending technique and also developed light occasional chairs, so-called *Laufsessel* (side chairs), that demonstrated a new language vis-à-vis the Biedermeier models from Boppard. In place of the laminates of glued veneer strips, Thonet now used glued rod-bundles, which allowed him to bend shapes not only within one plane but in any desired direction. This technical innovation was accompanied by a profound change in the shaping. The tube-shaped wooden rods in the newly developed models formed a knot as the only decoration in the backrest (see fig. 1). Thus from the vocabulary of the Rococo revival came the formal prototype for later production chairs.[12]

THE VIENNA WORKSHOP (1849–56)

Equipped with the new technical know-how for gluing rods, Thonet emerged from his anonymity within the Liechtenstein commission supported by the privilege of 1842. He became independent again in 1849 and established a workshop at Gumpendorfer Hauptstrasse 396. He now pursued several successful marketing strategies. In November 1850, he presented himself again to the Lower Austrian Trade Association, this time with rosewood furniture; a short while later he joined the association as an independent craftsman.[13] At the same time, Thonet began preparations to participate in the Exhibition of the Works of Industry of All Nations, held in 1851 at London's Crystal Palace. He presented expensive, luxury palisander furniture similar to the Liechtenstein models with brass and rosewood inlay and received the highest award in his class.[14] Desvignes, who had returned to England, purchased the exhibited pieces as a sign of his esteem. (They were bought back by the Thonet family after his death in 1883.)

By 1850 the Thonet workshop was primarily interested in developing a line of models starting with the Liechtenstein chairs.[15] The side chair with its twist motif in the backrest became the model for the light occasional chairs that Prince Schwarzenberg ordered for his garden palace in Vienna; these were later to be model number 1. Around 1849/50 the imperial household also ordered similar occasional furniture to furnish the Prague residence of Emperor Ferdinand I, who had gone into seclusion after abdicating during the Revolution in 1848; an extant example in the former Royal-Imperial Furniture Storage in Vienna shows that what Thonet produced later became model number 6 (cat. no. 5).[16] The furniture setting shown at the London exhibition corresponds to model number 9 (cat. no. 4). Along with their function as aristocratic occasional furniture, the light bentwood chairs were soon victorious in another realm: in 1857, model number 4 (cat. no. 3) was used to furnish Café Daum, in the heart of Vienna, and it became the standard chair of Viennese coffee houses.

Along with the development of new models, Michael Thonet strove to have the technique of rod-gluing, developed in the 1840s, protected through patents. He received a new patent on July 28, 1852, in the name of his sons, for the process of "giving wood various curves and forms by cutting and regluing." Again, only the technique of production, and not the actual production of furniture, was protected—which proved to be a point of contention for his competitors.

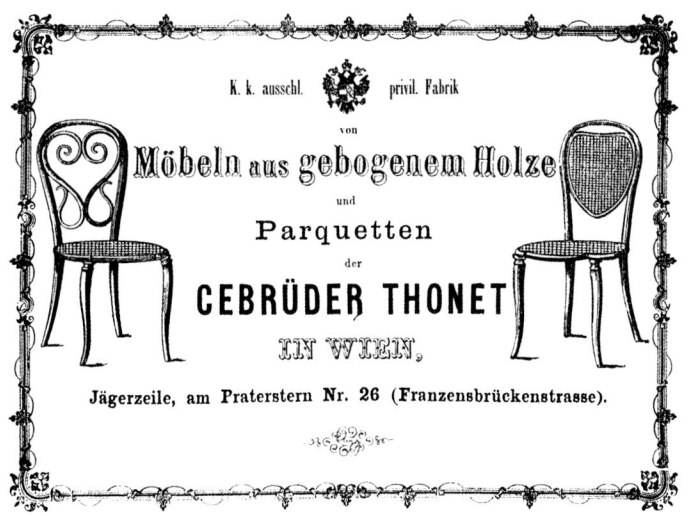

FIGURE 2
Advertisement for Gebrüder Thonet
Photo: *Lehmann's Wiener Adressbuch* (Vienna, 1860)

FIGURE 3
Advertisement for Josef Neyger firm
Photo: *Lehmann's Wiener Adressbuch* (Vienna, 1875)

In the winter of 1852, Thonet set up his first sales branch in the newly built Palais Montenuovo in the Strauchgasse. The workshop moved in 1853 to Mollardgasse 173, where before long a steam machine was installed.

On November 1, 1853, the fifty-seven-year-old Michael Thonet transferred the company—with a business capital of ten thousand standard florins, annual sales of twenty-four thousand florins, and forty-two workers—to his five sons: Franz (1820–1898), Michael (1824–1902), August (1829–1910), Josef (1830–1887), and Jakob (1841–1929). The firm was thereafter known as Gebrüder Thonet (Thonet Brothers). Michael, however, retained procurement powers, and was in no way considering retirement. On the contrary, this was merely a tactical maneuver in his competition with the Viennese cabinetmakers, who had tried to charge him with "trade interference" (i.e., he produced furniture, and not just furniture parts, from bent wood), and thus to pull out his economic foundation by contesting his patent as "lacking innovation." In fact, after 1850, competition had appeared in Vienna itself in the production of bentwood furniture. Along with Johann Weiss and Johann Kukol, we should mention here Josef Neyger, who consciously copied Thonet's models in advertisements and who continued to produce laminate chairs into the 1870s (see figs. 2, 3).[17]

Relief in the conflict with the cabinetmakers' guild came through the granting of factory authorization in 1855; at that time, the workshop already employed seventy workers and began to export to foreign countries. More difficult were Neyger's vehemently pursued contestations of Thonet's patent rights. For in the 1850s, Thonet no longer used the rod-gluing technique of the Liechtenstein models; rather, analysis of extant models from this time shows that the firm apparently used an improved layered-gluing technique. When it began to seem that Neyger's objection to the 1852 patent might be successful (in the end it failed), Michael Thonet hastily submitted a new patent application, and on July 10, 1856, received the privilege "to manufacture chairs and table legs from bent wood, the curvature of which is effected through steam or boiling liquids." This is the first protection by patent of Thonet's production of furniture out of bent wood. The technique of solid-wood bending did not go into production in Vienna, however, for the metropolis on the Danube had run its course as a production site.

THE FIRST FACTORIES (1856–69)

In order to expand further, it was necessary to make the step from craft to industrial production, and that meant moving the place of production to the source of raw materials, to the beech forests themselves. In the spring of 1856, Michael Thonet began to set up a factory in Koritschan, Moravia, a densely wooded region in which cheap labor was available. Vienna became the sales location and soon the center of an international sales network. The Mollardgasse workshop was closed down by 1858, and a new sales branch was set up in the Thonet residence in Leopoldstadt, Jägerzeile 26.

Production started up in Koritschan in 1857. In the beginning, semifinished wares were shipped to Vienna to be finished and assembled. Annual production amounted to ten thousand furniture pieces; by 1860, three hundred workers produced fifty thousand pieces. In 1861 Michael and August Thonet began to build a second factory in Bistritz, which started operations in 1862.

The technique of bending solid wood, patented in 1856, was ready for industrial production in the late 1850s, the danger that the wood would be stretched or torn in bending having been successfully prevented by the use of metal rails. At the same time, new models were developed, such as chair model number 14 (cat. no. 7), whose backrest was formed by only two bent rods in parallel arcs. It consists of only six individual parts, and is still mass-produced with the smallest expense of any model. The fundamental goal was to construct all models out of standardized individual parts—chair legs, seats, etc.—in order to produce, assemble, and package them as economically as possible: thirty-six chairs of model number 14 could be packed in a crate only one cubic meter large.

In 1859, Gebrüder Thonet published, in addition to their advertisements (see fig. 2) in various daily newspapers and journals, the first known catalog page, showing twenty-six models. Along with chairs, these included armchairs, settees, and tables. In the increasingly complex Thonet enterprise, the use of model numbers served to simplify communication between the factories, the sales branches, and the retail trade. For each chair type—in accordance with the historicist idea of a set—armchairs and settees were developed with the same model numbers and with corresponding motifs for the backrest. Markings also served to distinguish models produced by the Thonets from those of their competitors (much like porcelain marks). Since the founding of the workshop in 1849, the pieces had been marked with the company stamp or registered trademark, which today represent important documents for dating technical developments.[18]

Around 1860, a bentwood rocking chair was introduced as a new model. "Rocking Armchair No. 1" embodied a formal reckoning with the metal rocker of R. W. Winfield, which had been exhibited at the London international exhibitions in 1851 and 1862.[19] Bentwood chairs derived from aristocratic side chairs had found their first home primarily in large-scale seating arrangements; the rocking chair now became the first bentwood furniture developed for middle-class living rooms. This was the potential clientele that had to be addressed in the last decades of the nineteenth century.

With the establishment of factory production in the early 1860s—especially with the development of model number 14, the so-called "chair for mass consumption" *(Konsumsessel),* Thonet created classics of anonymous furniture design that are exemplary even today. In contrast to the luxury furniture Thonet presented in 1851, only the industrial product series was displayed (and enthusiastically received) at the London international exhibition of 1862. The catalog describes the chairs as "combining in a remarkable degree lightness with strength, and being produced at singularly

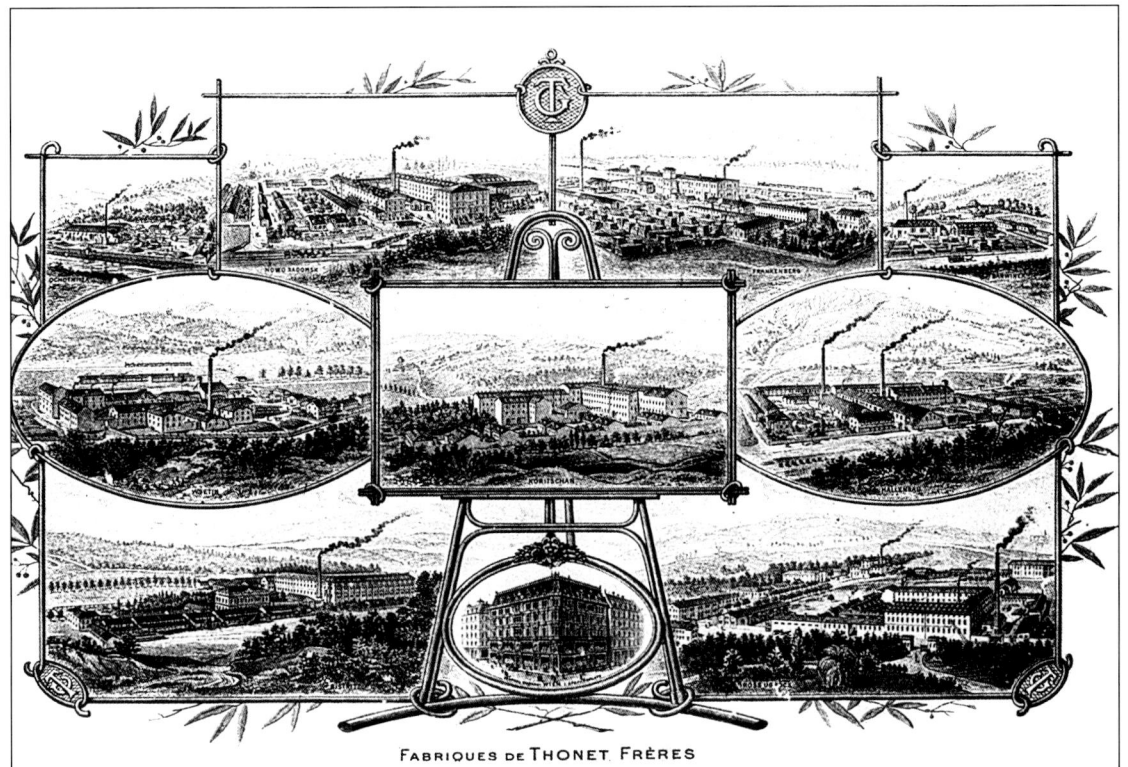

FIGURE 4
Factories of Gebrüder Thonet, c. 1885
Courtesy Archiv Gebrüder Thonet GmbH, Frankenberg

small cost. . . . The designs are generally graceful and good, the great purpose of 'use' being always kept in view."[20] The forms themselves reflected the demands of industrial production, which the German architect and theoretician Gottfried Semper had articulated in 1852 in *Wissenschaft, Industrie und Kunst* (Science, industry, and art):

> A product for the market must now allow the most general use possible and may not express any other conditions than those that the goal and material of the object allow. The place is not given for which it is intended, nor are the characteristics of the person known, whose property it will become. It must therefore have no individual character and local color, but rather it must have qualities which enable it to fit into any environment harmoniously.[21]

After the start-up of the factory in Bistritz in 1862, eight hundred workers were producing eighty thousand pieces of bentwood furniture annually; the largest portion of these was chairs, and of these the largest fraction was model number 14. The expansion was only beginning: in 1865, the wooded estate of Gross-Ugrócz (now in Hungary) was purchased, and another furniture factory set up. As in Koritschan, this factory supplied semifinished pieces until workers were thoroughly trained. In May 1867, they signed a contract for the supply of lumber with the Belgian Société civile de Wsetin, and acquired a steam-driven saw in nearby Hallenkau, where another factory was founded in 1868. To avoid having Russian import tariffs placed on their products, a factory was founded in 1880 in Novoradomsk, in Russian Poland. In 1889 a last plant was set up in densely-wooded Frankenberg, in Hesse, Germany (see fig. 4). By 1900, six thousand workers were producing four thousand pieces of bentwood furniture per day (see figs. 5 and 6).

The working conditions in the Thonet factories were in line with the economic and social expectations of the nineteenth century. The production process was divided into steps through planned division of labor, so that unskilled workers from the agricultural regions of Moravia, Silesia,

FIGURES 5 AND 6
Workers in the Moravian Thonet factory, after 1900
Courtesy Archiv Gebrüder Thonet GmbH, Frankenberg

Hungary, or Poland could be put to work in the factories without special training. Men worked generally with the raw wood, and in the sawing and bending processes, while women and children worked at staining, caning, and packing. The workday lasted, on average, twelve to fourteen hours. The social responsibility of the enterprise towards its workers can be seen in a variety of charitable and leisure foundations. Among these were health insurance, workers' residences, factory schools, and benefits for widows and orphans, as well as savings and cooperative associations, a factory fire department, and the workers' own music band.[22]

Keeping pace with the expansion of production was Gebrüder Thonet's international sales system. In 1861 a new sales center was set up at Leopoldstadt 586, near the Franzensbrücke in Vienna, and a sales branch was opened in Budapest. In 1862 a branch was established in London as a result of the second London International Exhibition. Two decades later, Gebrüder Thonet built their residence and headquarters on one of the most central and desirable lots in Vienna, on the Stephansplatz (see fig. 7). The enterprise eventually had access to sales offices in Amsterdam, Barcelona, Berlin, Brno, Brussels, Chicago, Frankfurt, Graz, Hamburg, Madrid, Marseilles, Milan, Moscow, Munich, Naples, New York, Odessa, Paris, Prague, Rome, and Saint Petersburg.

FIGURE 7

Thonet residence, Stephansplatz, Vienna, c. 1880

Courtesy Archiv Gebrüder Thonet GmbH, Frankenberg

This worldwide expansion of Gebrüder Thonet did not remain without competition, however; in eastern Moravia, with its rich reservoirs of both wood and labor, appeared an adversary who could not be shaken off by introducing new technology or more favorable production sites. The struggle for market share in the decades leading up to World War I was carried out above all in the realm of marketing and in the constantly expanding variety of products offered.

JACOB & JOSEF KOHN—INDUSTRIAL COMPETITION (1869–1900)

Around 1850, the businessman Jacob Kohn (1814–1884) started to trade in lumber in Wsetin; demand increased through the construction of railroads and the building boom of the *Gründerzeit*, the rapid industrial growth of mid- to late-nineteenth-century Germany and Austria. Kohn set up a steam-driven saw, participated in the construction of a match-stick factory, and founded a glass factory in the 1860s.[23] Spurred on by the success of Gebrüder Thonet, which had moved into the area of Hallenkau/Wsetin in 1867, Kohn recognized bentwood furniture as a lucrative way to utilize the rich lumber resources. In addition, he had the advantage of entering directly into an industrial technology, circumventing the tedious process of perfecting his craft. So in 1867, together with his son Josef, Kohn founded a bentwood furniture company, apparently beginning production in the glass factory a short while later with workers hired away from Thonet. The patented protection of Thonet's production process remained an obstacle. The 1856 patent was to expire in 1869, but like the Viennese competitors of the 1850s, Kohn had already tried to contest it before then on the basis of lack of innovation. It was apparent that the recommendation of the Polytechnical Institute in Vienna would be against Gebrüder Thonet, so the firm decided voluntarily to forego the renewal of its patent on December 10, 1869. The door now stood open for numerous new bentwood furniture makers.

In contrast to the Paris international exhibition of 1867, where Gebrüder Thonet could still display their wares without competition, at the Vienna international exhibition in 1873 (see fig. 8) they were joined by several other firms: Jacob & Josef Kohn; Josef Neyger, who still produced in the obsolete layer-gluing technique; D. G. Fischel Söhne, founded in 1870 in Niemes, Silesia (now Mimon, Czech Republic), which soon became the third largest bentwood furniture maker; and the Seemann & Teubler company from Bohemia.

Kohn progressed rapidly in the 1870s. The factory in Wsetin was rebuilt after a fire in 1870; affiliates were established in Kelsch, and in Warsaw and Porembo in 1873–74; and new factories were founded in Teschen in 1871, in Cracow in 1872, in Czenstochau in 1878 (which was moved in 1884 to Novoradomsk), and, finally, in Halleschau in 1890. At the turn of the century, Kohn's production capacity of four thousand pieces per day matched that of Gebrüder Thonet, and the annual consumption of beechwood amounted to forty thousand cubic meters. Their vast sales network was modeled on Thonet's, with offices in Antwerp, Barcelona, Berlin, Budapest, Cologne, London, Madrid, Milan, Naples, Nuremberg, Paris, Rome, Saint Petersburg, and Warsaw.

Though the Kohn company's slogan "semper sursum" (ever onward), like Michael Thonet's principle "to bend or break," confirmed an aggressive business policy, the struggle for market share no longer depended solely on production figures, but rather on expansion of the product lines. Thonet's first catalog page from 1859 offered twenty-six different models of chairs, settees, and a few tables; in 1866 there were seventy, and the catalog page printed for the Vienna international exhibition in 1873 offered eighty bentwood models (see fig. 9). Along with the new chair designs

FIGURE 8
Gebrüder Thonet exhibition display, Vienna international exhibition, 1873
Courtesy Archiv Gebrüder Thonet GmbH, Frankenberg

and the rocking chair, there were specialized pieces such as children's furniture and revolving and folding chairs intended in part for offices. It is clear in the advertisements from these years that J. & J. Kohn, like earlier competitors of the 1850s, copied Thonet's product line and models (fig. 10). In the earliest known Kohn catalog—probably printed for the Philadelphia Centennial Exposition of 1876—there are chair-and-settee sets as well as tables, rocking chairs, and children's furniture.

Around 1877/78 Kohn took the initiative, however, and directed the production of bentwood furniture into a new area of sales. The goal was to take over the middle-class living room, as Thonet had come to dominate large-scale seating arrangements. This meant reworking the historicist style of home decor; the models received a square cross-section, as in traditional cabinetmaker furniture, as well as lavish padding. To become suitable for the salon, the motifs of revival styles had to be incorporated, so the company set up its own drawing studio. In addition, to satisfy this clientele's desire for "complete" furnishings, a factory was set up in 1890 in Holleschau to produce chests. Thus, J. & J. Kohn offered residential furniture matching the tastes of the late nineteenth century, as well as "classical" bentwood furniture. Gebrüder Thonet followed suit: in the catalogs of 1886 and 1888, the number of models had not only grown from 294 to 339, but there were now chair sets in neo-Gothic and neo-Renaissance styles, as well as opulently padded "salon sets." At the same time, there were always additional types of furniture offered: the product line extended to beds, daybeds, and baby carriages; to mirror frames (cat. no. 27), washstands, and other bathroom furniture; to office and theater seating (cat. no. 62); and finally to sports equipment (rings, tennis rackets, and skis) and garden furniture.

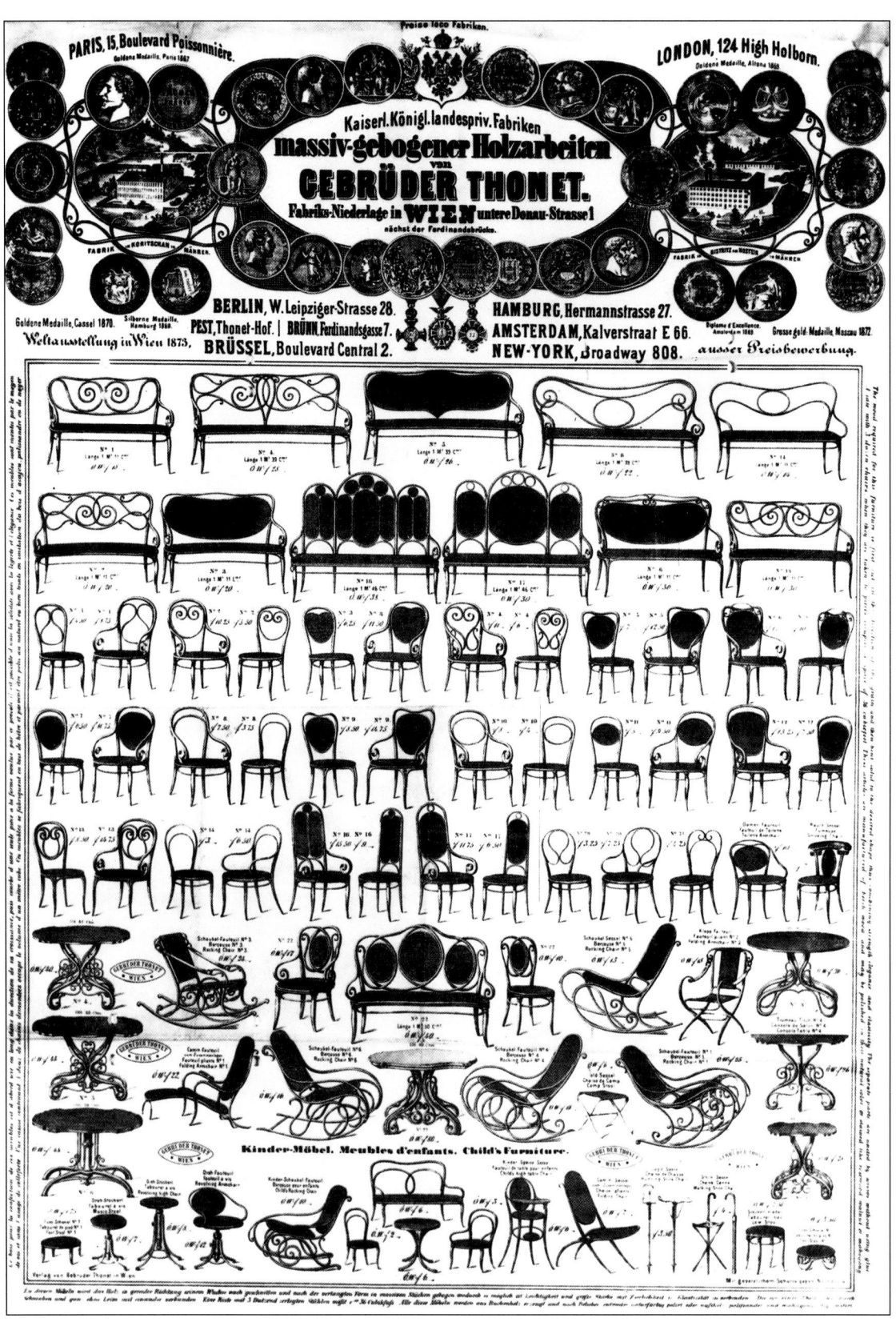

FIGURE 9
Gebrüder Thonet catalog page for the Vienna international exhibition, 1873
Courtesy Archiv Gebrüder Thonet GmbH, Frankenberg

Meanwhile, technical innovations in the production of bentwood furniture continued. J. & J. Kohn concentrated on simplifying assembly. In 1877 a removable cane seat for chairs was presented at the Vienna Furniture Hall, an "angular closure" was introduced, and a more stable construction of Thonet's classic model number 14 was propagated. The company also presented a convertible baby carriage in which an infant could sit at a dining table as well as be wheeled around.[24] Thonet soon included this model in their lineup as well (cat. no. 35).

August Thonet, the inventor among the brothers, had already presented an experimental chair made out of an "endless loop" (a single, twenty-two foot rod) of bent wood at the Paris exhibition in 1867.[25] He developed a machine for bending seat rings and veneer wooden seats as alternatives to seats of woven cane. Obviously spurred on by a chair patented in 1874 by the American Isaak Sargent,[26] he experimented with chairs of bent solid wood boards.[27] This American bentwood furniture tradition, reaching back to the Bostonian Samuel Gragg (1772–1855), saw experiment and industrialization in the hands of the Heywoods of Gardner, Massachusetts, who had begun in 1826 to produce solid wood chairs, especially of the Windsor type. Heywood Brothers & Company soon established a factory and developed special bending machines. When Franz Thonet visited the American competitor's plant at the time of the Centennial Exposition, his reaction found its way into the company's chronicle, for he observed: "I must tell you candidly that you have the best machinery in the world for bending wood that I have ever seen, and I will say that I have seen and experimented a great deal in the bending of wood."[28]

This meeting demonstrates that bentwood furniture had become a transatlantic manufacture and a worldwide commodity. More than fifty companies were producing bentwood furniture in the 1890s.[29] For Gebrüder Thonet, the year 1896, the centennial of Michael Thonet's birth, presented an occasion for looking back at the company's traditions,[30] and the impulse for a new direction in the industry came from Kohn.

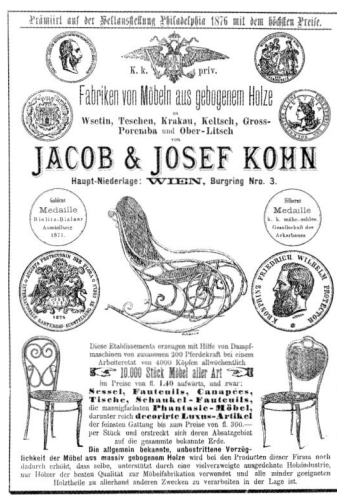

FIGURE 10

Advertisement for Jacob & Josef Kohn

Photo: *Lehmann's Wiener Adressbuch* (Vienna, 1877)

BENTWOOD FURNITURE AS A DESIGNERS' PRODUCT (1900–14)

At the Paris Exposition Universelle in 1900, the Kohn company presented bentwood furniture designed by Gustav Siegel (1880–1970), a student of the School of Applied Arts in Vienna, and received the grand prize for the pieces exhibited (fig. 11).[31] The Viennese Jugendstil started with the ideas of the English Arts and Crafts movement and parallelled the Art Nouveau; its objectives—to shape the entire human environment artistically and in a contemporary way—spurred Kohn to convert bentwood furniture from anonymous industrial products into a challenging medium for Viennese architects and designers, and thus into an "applied art." Kohn's products were now displayed at arts and crafts exhibitions and presented in related journals. Even the company's advertisements, catalogs, and sales sites changed their appearance to partake of the Jugendstil. Siegel remained on staff as designer at Kohn, but his teacher Josef Hoffmann (1870–1956) and Koloman Moser (1868-1918) also began to develop bent wood designs for the company.[32] In 1902 the architect and teacher Otto Wagner (1841–1918) commissioned Kohn to make chairs for the telegraph office Die Zeit, which he was designing. From 1907 on he also turned to Siegel's chair for the Exposition Universelle (cat. no. 46), for example in the armchairs he used in the Postal Savings Bank (Postsparkasse) building in Vienna. Hoffmann also had Kohn make the chairs for his Cabaret Fledermaus in Vienna, 1907, and the for dining room of the Sanatorium Westend in Purkersdorf, 1904. Kohn added these to their catalog (cat. nos. 57, 50). It is of interest to note that the designers themselves only placed bentwood furniture in their buildings in the traditional format of large-scale seating, while the Kohn company itself, as seen in its historicist salon furniture, was striving to offer products for bourgeois living spaces. It is in this light that we must view their models—even Hoffmann's *Sitzmaschine* (sitting machine) of 1905 (cat. no. 53), and the house he designed for Kohn for the Vienna Art Show of 1908, which was entirely furnished in bent wood.

Gebrüder Thonet only turned to designer furniture around 1904–05, when the company assigned Wagner's student and Postsparkasse-colleague Marcel Kammerer (1879–1969) to design bentwood furniture. He reworked his experiences with Wagner's models for the Postparkasse and the standard for bentwood furniture developed contemporaneously by Siegel and Hoffmann. Within the company's catalog—with close to twelve hundred models by 1904—the modernist designs were seen, like the historicist ones earlier, as a product line for a specific public. But they also published specialized catalogs with architect's designs, just as in advertising in general they targeted the actual public addressed. Examples of this practice are catalogs conceived specifically for the American market after 1900; they contained no designer models, but rather a multitude of historicist furniture, more or less of the Windsor type, that could not be found at all in the European offerings, but which were standard offerings of the American chairmakers the Heywood Brothers. The designer models also consciously followed the general stylistic development of the Viennese Jugendstil furniture; thus, Otto Prutscher (1873–1959) developed a heavy, rather classicist chair for Thonet after 1910, while Hoffmann designed a decorative, playful arrangement for the Kohn display at the German Trade Association Exposition in Cologne in 1914.

FIGURE 11
Jacob & Josef Kohn exhibition display at Exposition Universelle, Paris, 1900, showing models by Gustav Siegel, in *J. & J. Kohn Katalog*, 1904
Courtesy Archiv C. Witt-Dörring, Vienna

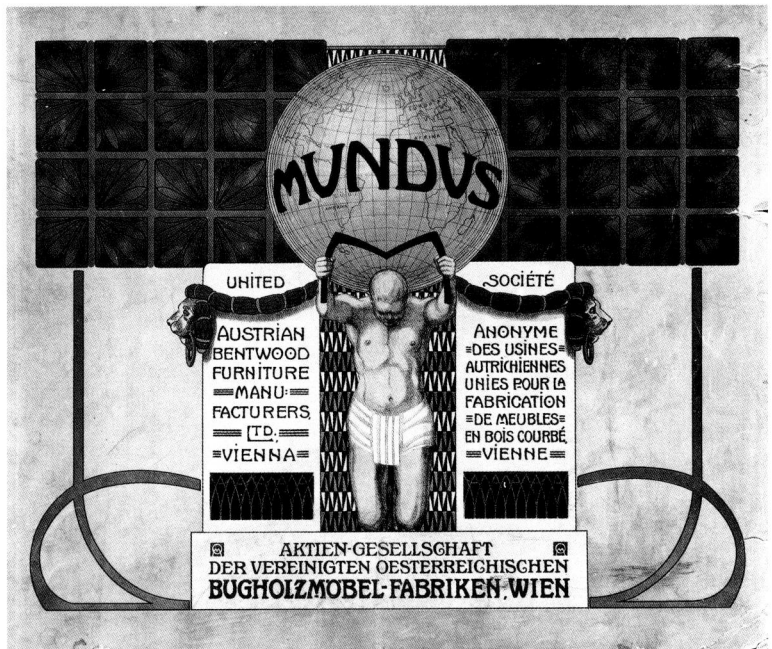

FIGURE 12

Cover page, Mundus AG catalog, c. 1907/10

Courtesy Archiv P. Asenbaum, Vienna

MERGERS AND THE MUNDUS CORPORATION (1907–22)

While the direction of Gebrüder Thonet after 1900 gradually changed over to grandchildren of Michael Thonet, the J. & J. Kohn company in 1901 was incorporated as the Erste österreichische Aktiengesellschaft zur Erzeugung von Möbeln aus gebogenem Holz Jacob und Josef Kohn. The continuing increase in production figures of the two market leaders forced out the majority of small bentwood furniture makers. Thus, Leopold Pilzer (1871–1959), a partner of Rudolf Weill & Co.,[33] was able, with the aid of the Österreichische Creditanstalt bank, on August 20, 1907, to join together sixteen small bentwood furniture makers into the Mundus corporation (see fig. 12). In 1914, at the beginning of World War I, the company took over the majority of shares of Kohn, forming the Kohn-Mundus holding company, into which, during the economic turmoil that followed the war, Gebrüder Thonet was finally integrated. After 1922, Pilzer directed a corporate empire, the Thonet-Mundus holding company, with over ten thousand workers and twenty production sites in Austria, Germany, and the successor states of the former Danube monarchy.[34] In the 1920s, the future of furniture design no longer lay in bent wood, but in bent metal, plywood, and plastics. From the small-town shop of a cabinetmaker to an international conglomerate, the evolution of the bentwood furniture industry recapitulates the history of the industrial revolution itself.

NOTES

1. I wish to express my gratitude to some of my long-time colleagues for their fascinating exchange of ideas: Alessandro Alverá, Vienna; Dr. Paul Asenbaum, Vienna; Dr. Helmut W. Lang, Österreichische Nationalbibliothek, Vienna; Alexander von Vegesack, Vitra Design Museum, Weil am Rhein; Christopher Wilk, Victoria and Albert Museum, London; and Dr. Christian Witt-Dörring, Museum für angewandte Kunst, Vienna. Thanks also go to Gebrüder Thonet GmbH, Frankenberg, for their help in supplying photographs.

2. See Nikolaus Pevsner, "The First Plywood Furniture," *Architectural Review* 84, no. 501 (August 1938), p. 75ff.

3. *Ausführlicher Bericht über die Allgemeine deutsche Industrie-Ausstellung zu Mainz 1842* (Darmstadt, 1843), p. 113: Thonet exhibited six "elastic mahogany chairs for 47 fl.," two chairs for forty-two florins, and a small table with a spiral column. His workshop employed twenty to twenty-five workers at that time.

4. Ibid., p. 112; see also the report on Kertell in *Monatsblätter des Gewerbevereins des Herzogtums Hessen* 1 (1842), p. 17ff.

5. *Amtlicher Bericht über die Allgemeine deutsche Gewerbe-Ausstellung* (Berlin, 1844) p. 103, no. 2793.

6. W. C. W. Blumenbach, *Wiener Kunst und Gewerbefreund oder der neueste Wiener Geschmack* (Vienna, 1825), intro.

7. *Bericht zur dritten allgemeinen österreichischen Gewerbeprodukten-Ausstellung* (Vienna, 1845), pp. 735, 750.

8. *Verhandlungen und Mitteilungen des Niederösterreichischen Gewerbevereins* 8 (1843), pp. 28–34.

9. *Bericht der ersten österreichischen Gewerbeprodukten-Ausstellung* (Vienna, 1835), p. 315; *Bericht der zweiten österreichischen Gewerbeprodukten-Ausstellung* (Vienna, 1839), p. 387.

10. *Sitz-Gelegenheiten, Bugholz- und Stahlrohrmöbel von Thonet*, exh. cat. Germanisches Nationalmuseums (Nürnberg, 1989), fig. 69; one piece is now in the Museum für angewandte Kunst, Vienna, and two are privately owned.

11. See Marianne Zweig, *Zweites Rokoko, Innenräume und Hausrat in Wien 1830 bis 1860* (Vienna, 1924); Eva B. Ottillinger, "The 'Kaiser-Salon' and the Beginnings of the Rococo Revival in Vienna," *Furniture History* 27 (1991), pp. 137–47.

12. On the technology, see Alessandro Alverá, "Michael Thonet and the Development of Bent-Wood Furniture: From Workshop to Factory Production," in Derek E. Ostergard, ed., *Bent Wood and Metal Furniture: 1850–1946*, exh. cat. American Federation of Arts (New York, 1987), pp. 33–52.

13. *Verhandlungen und Mitteilungen des Niederösterreichischen Gewerbevereins* 47 (1850), p. 372.

14. *The Crystal Palace Illustrated Catalogue, Art Journal Special Number* (London, 1851), p. 296. They are located today in part in the family collection and in the Ton Museum in Bistritz; see *Sitz-Gelegenheiten* (note 10), nos 21–25.

15. The prince and his wife wanted to order additional chairs around 1850. It was only then that they discovered through a letter from Desvignes that their chairs were not from Leistler, but rather a "certain Mr. Thonet"; this is the only reference to Thonet in the Liechtenstein Archives in Vienna.

16. See *Sitz-Gelegenheiten* (note 10), no. 20.

17. Helmut W. Lang, "Auch im Kampf gegen die Konkurrenz. Thonets Motto: Biegen oder Brechen," *Das Wilde Biedermeier, 1800–1848, Parnass Sonderheft* 4 (1987), pp. 56–67, and "Die Bugholztechniken Michael Thonets und seiner Konkurrenten" in *Sitz-Gelegenheiten* (note 10), pp. 67–74.

18. From 1849 on, the stamp "Thonet Wien Gump. 396" was used, followed about 1853 by "GB Thonet," "Thonet Wien," or "GT"; after the 1856 patent for solid wood techniques, paper labels were affixed with "k.k. ausschl. priv. u. landesbef. Fab. massiv gebogener Holz-Arbeiten von Gebrüder Thonet Wien"; finally, after 1881 came the protected trademark "Thonet Wien." See Peter W. Ellenberg, "Schutzmarken, Etiketten und sonstige Markierungen," in *Sitz-Gelegenheiten* (note 10), pp. 127–137.

19. Ibid., cat. no. 113; see also Eva B. Ottillinger, "Thonet als Vorbild—Vorbilder für Thonet: Das Bugholzmöbel und die Zeitgenossen," in *Sitz-Gelegenheiten* (note 10), pp. 55–56; and note 12, p. 210.

20. *Art Journal Illustrated Catalogue* (London, 1862), p. 291.

21. Gottfried Semper, *Wissenschaft, Industrie und Kunst* (Braunschweig, 1852; rev. ed., Mainz, 1966), p. 40.

22. See *Gebrüder Thonet, Institutionen zum Wohle der Arbeiter, Beitrag zur Ausstellung für Unfall-Verhütung* (Berlin and Vienna, 1889). The J. & J. Kohn company provided similar resources.

23. Ladislav Baletka, "Das Holz als Phänomen der Industrialisierung Ostmährens," in *Sitz-Gelegenheiten* (note 10), pp. 111–18. On the Kohn firm in general, see also: *Die Grossindustrie in Österreich*, vol. 3 (Vienna, 1898), pp. 320–22, and vol. 1 (rev. ed. Vienna, 1908), pp. 382–385; and "Erste österreichische Actien-Gesellschaft zur Erzeugung von Möbeln aus gebogenem Holz Jacob und Josef Kohn," in *Historisch-biographische Blätter (Industrie, Handel und Gewerbe)* (Berlin and Vienna, 1902).

24. *Wiener Möbelhalle* (Vienna, 1877), p. 2ff.

25. *Sitz-Gelegenheiten* (note 10), no. 100.

26. See Siegfried Giedion, *Mechanization Takes Command* (New York, 1969), p. 383.

27. *Sitz-Gelegenheiten* (note 10), nos. 103, 107–109; see also Alexander von Vegesack, *Das Thonet Buch* (Munich, 1987), pp. 97–102.

28. Richard N. Greenwood, *The Five Heywood Brothers (1826–1951)* (New York, 1951), p. 13. In the United States, there appears to have been an intense interchange between basket-furniture production and bent-wood technology; this is illustrated by the interrelationship of the Heywood Brothers and Wakefield Company. Wicker furniture since the mid-nineteenth century was produced around a weight-bearing construction of bent rattan or hickory. See E. B. Ottillinger, *Korbmöbel* (Salzburg/Vienna, 1990), pp. 73–81.

29. Wilhelm Exner, *Das Biegen des Holzes* (3rd ed., Weimar, 1893; 1st ed. 1876), pp. 29–31. See also *Die Grossindustrie in Österreich*, vol. 3 (note 23), p. 306.

30. See *Michael Thonet, Ein Gedenkblatt aus Anlass der 100. Wiederkehr seines Geburtstages*, ed. and pub. by Gebrüder Thonet (Vienna, 1896).

31. Jacob & Josef Kohn had already made furniture conceived by the Viennese architect Adolf Loos in 1899 for the Café Museum, but these models did not go into serial production; see Ottillinger (note 19), p. 59ff.

32. Ibid., pp. 60–62; see Christian Witt-Dörring, "Bent Wood Production and the Viennese Avant-garde: Thonet Brothers and J. and J. Kohn, 1899–1914," in Ostergard (note 12), pp. 95–120.

33. See *Die Grossindustrie in Österreich*, vol. 3 (note 23), pp. 328–330.

34. For more on the firms involved, see B. Otto, "Entwicklung der mitteleuropäischen Bugholzmöbelindustrie," diss. Friedrich Alexander Universität (Erlangen, 1931), p. 82ff.

CATALOG OF THE EXHIBITION

All of the firms and designers of bentwood furniture included in the catalog are Austrian, with the exception of the American Samuel Gragg (cat. no. 1). Dating industrially produced furniture poses a challenge. We have relied on the appearance of the model in company catalogs as the primary source for the date of a piece. The labels on some pieces also may help us limit the period in which they were manufactured. Many objects have been assigned dates based on an assessment of their style. None of these factors, however, determines exactly when a given piece in the Steinfeld collection was made, and therefore for most objects we have noted a period of probable manufacture. The corporate mergers of the 1920s complicate nomenclature and dating of firms. This catalog lists Gebrüder Thonet as being in operation from 1853 until 1921, when it became a joint-stock company and was then absorbed into the holding company Mundus AG. (For simplicity's sake, however, and because many pieces are dated uncertainly, the appendix to this catalog uses the term Gebrüder Thonet for pieces made between the world wars.) In entitling the furniture, cues were taken from the sales catalogs in which they first appeared. Exceptions have been made where shifts in usage—or flawed translations into English— make the period terms unwieldy.

Most of the furniture reproduced in this catalog is housed in the Shelby Williams Industries Chair Museum in Morristown, Tennessee.

1 / ARMCHAIR

Designer and manufacturer: Samuel Gragg (1772– c. 1855), c. 1808
Oak, ash, maple, beech, painted decoration, metal braces
34 3/8 x 21 1/8 x 26 in. (87. 3 x 53.7 x 66 cm)

Well before Michael Thonet developed the technology to mass-produce furniture from bent solid wood, chair makers in both Europe and the United States were experimenting with innovative wood-bending techniques. In 1808, the Boston furniture maker Samuel Gragg received a patent for an "elastic chair." In the following year he advertised his recently designed "Chairs and settees, with elastic backs and bottoms" suitable for use in "drawing-rooms, parlors, halls and other apartments." In this graceful example, parallel lengths of bent wood form the vertical elements in the chair's back and alternating ribs in the seat. These curved members are secured in place by the horizontal crest rail and front and back elements of the seat frame. Known as a "fancy chair" for its painted decoration, this example retains its original painted peacock feather centered on the crest rail and stylized leaves on the front seat rail. Gragg's furniture was advertised as being "very strong, light and airy," qualities that would become hallmarks of Michael Thonet's bentwood furniture in succeeding decades.

2 / SIDE CHAIR

Designer and manufacturer: Michael Thonet (1796–1871), 1836/40
Wood laminate, walnut veneer, upholstery (front stretcher missing)
33½ x 17 x 18½ in. (85.1 x 43 x 47 cm)
Collection of Shelby Williams Industries, Inc.

Revolutionary technology was allied to the contemporary Biedermeier aesthetic in this chair, sometimes referred to as the Boppard chair after the city where Michael Thonet was born and established a furniture workshop in 1819. Lightweight and lyrical in outline, it is one of the earliest forms made by Thonet using bent laminates. The legs, side seat rails, and back stiles are composed of a sandwich of thin veneers cut in the direction of the grain, made flexible through immersion in hot glue, and bent in molds to form the skeleton of the chair. The two sides were joined with the front and back seat rails and laminated crest rail and splat, the whole veneered with fine-grained walnut in emulation of the prevailing Biedermeier taste.

Thonet's ambitions were not satisfied by the market offered by Boppard alone. Encouraged by the Austrian chancellor, Klemens von Metternich, Thonet left Boppard am Rhein in 1842 to settle in Vienna. In the cosmopolitan heart of the Austro-Hungarian empire, Thonet's technological innovations came to the attention of the English architect Peter Hubert Desvignes (1804–1883), who arranged for him to produce elaborate parquet floors and lightweight bentwood chairs for the Viennese palace of Prince Alois Josef I of Liechtenstein. At the same time, Thonet continued to experiment with new methods for bending wood, laying the groundwork for an independent workshop in 1849 and his firm's phenomenal expansion in the second half of the nineteenth century.

3 / SIDE CHAIR, MODEL NO. 4
Designer: Michael Thonet
(1796–1871), 1848/50
Manufacturer: Gebrüder Thonet
(1853–1921), late 1870s/1881
Beech, cane
36 x 16⅝ x 20½ in. (91.4 x 42.2 x 52.1 cm)

The 1850s was a period of enormous change in patronage, technology, and business organization for Michael Thonet. After achieving his independence from the workshop of the Viennese cabinetmaker Carl Leistler in 1849, Thonet continued to benefit from the patronage of Vienna's princely and aristocratic clientele, fashioning chairs along the lines of those provided for the prince of Liechtenstein (see Ottillinger, fig. 1). In 1853 Michael Thonet restructured his company, making his five sons equal partners in what became Gebrüder Thonet (Thonet Brothers). He and his sons were granted Austrian citizenship in June 1856; one month later, Gebrüder Thonet received a patent "to manufacture chairs and table legs from bent wood, the curvature of which is effected through steam or boiling liquids." At the same time business expanded into mass consumption, for in 1857 Thonet received his first large commission for a public space—to supply bentwood-and-cane side chairs for the Café Daum, a fashionable meeting place in the heart of Vienna. The coffeehouse was an important institution in Viennese city life, a forum for social life, discussion, playing billiards, and reading newspapers. Thonet's newly designed bentwood chairs were durable, lightweight, inexpensive, hygienic, and ideally suited to the shifting seating arrangements and heavy use to which café and restaurant furniture was subjected. The chairs for Café Daum were identified as model number 4 in Gebrüder Thonet's first single-page catalog of 1859. Like many of the firm's pieces, this model was modified in the course of production to strengthen it and make it more durable. The circular leg brace below the seat in this example first appeared in the 1866 broadsheet catalog while the pair of side braces connecting the seat and chair back was introduced in the late 1870s.

GEBRÜDER THONET PAPER LABEL, IN USE C. 1862/1881

4 / SIDE CHAIR, MODEL NO. 9
Designer: Michael Thonet
(1796–1871), c. 1851
Manufacturer: Gebrüder Thonet
(1853–1921), c. 1855
Glued rod bundles, cane
35¾ x 16⅜ x 20⅝ in. (90.8 x 42.1 x 52.4 cm)

Thonet's bentwood furniture first came to international attention in 1851, when he entered a selection of his luxury furnishings at London's "Exhibition of the Works of Industry of All Nations," the first of the great world fairs of the nineteenth century. Thonet's display at the Crystal Palace comprised tables and seating furniture, including an example of this model, in palisander inlaid with brass. The bifurcated front legs and the triangular reserve in the knees of this chair were inspired by the Rococo-revival upholstered chairs Thonet first created for the prince of Liechtenstein in the 1840s (see Ottillinger, fig. 1). In this example, which must date within a few years of the design's London debut because of the use of glued rod bundles, Thonet used six lengths of bent laminate to form the principal outline of the chair, inserting a laminate loop at each knee to accentuate its visual lightness and elegance.

5 / ARMCHAIR, MODEL NO. 6
Designer: Michael Thonet
(1796–1871), c. 1850/1855
Manufacturer: Gebrüder Thonet
(1853–1921), c. 1890s
Beech, cane
38¾ x 21½ x 23⅜ in. (98.4 x 54.6 x 56.9 cm)
Collection of Shelby Williams Industries, Inc.

A chair of this form (without the ring stretcher) first appeared in Thonet's broadsheet advertisement for 1859, but the seeds of its design were planted almost a decade earlier. The construction of the legs and the pierced reserve of the knees relate to the side chair first exhibited in 1851 in London's Crystal Palace exhibition (see cat. no. 4). The scrolling loops of bentwood ribbons embracing the chair back were first seen in a chair designed by Michael Thonet around 1850—for the former Austrian Emperor Ferdinand I, in exile in Prague—and are characteristic of the prevailing Rococo-revival style seen in Thonet furniture of the 1840s and early 1850s.

Thonet recognized early the importance of foreign markets for the growth of his business and considered international exhibitions essential to his strategy for increasing overseas consumption. After the London presentation in 1851, Gebrüder Thonet entered international exhibitions in Munich (1854), Paris (1855, 1867, 1878), London (1862, 1871), Vienna (1873), and Philadelphia (1876). At the same time, sales offices were opened, first in London in 1862, followed shortly by Paris, Hamburg, Berlin, and Rotterdam. By 1862, almost two-thirds of Thonet's bentwood chairs were being sold outside Austria. This chair bears a label for the Paris office of Thonet Frères at 15, Boulevard Poissonnière, and the instructions, "To keep our furniture in good condition, please tighten the screws and nuts three or four times a year."

6 / ARMCHAIR, MODEL NO. 2
Designer: Michael Thonet
(1796–1871), c. 1854
Manufacturer: Gebrüder Thonet
(1853–1921), late 19th/early 20th century
Beech, cane
37½ x 20⅝ x 23½ in. (95.3 x 52.4 x 59.7 cm)

7 / SIDE CHAIR, MODEL NO. 14
Designer: Michael Thonet (1796–1871), c. 1857/1858
Manufacturer: Gebrüder Thonet (1853–1921), c. 1881/1921
Beech, cane
35½ x 16¾ x 20¾ in. (90.2 x 42.6 x 52.7 cm)

Among the best-selling bentwood chair models, this "chair for mass consumption" was found in both public and private spaces. In its most pared-down form (without the two side braces), this chair was assembled from six pieces of wood simply held together with screws and nuts. Despite the anonymous nature of this chair's design, it shows clear stylistic links with Biedermeier-period chairs. The double loop of the chair back, formed from two separate pieces of wood, is seen in a design and in extant chairs by Josef Ulrich Danhauser (1780–1829). Until the establishment of Thonet's workshops and factories, Danhauser and his son directed the largest furniture and furnishings workshop in Vienna, supplying furniture, metalwork, glass, and accessories. A page from a sketchbook of about 1820/25 from Danhauser's factory shows a design for a traditionally carved and veneered chair designated number 18 (see Zelleke, fig. 1): its double crescent back may have inspired Michael Thonet in the creation of this bentwood classic.

8 / SIDE CHAIR

Unknown manufacturer (Austrian), c. 1860
Beech, wood laminate, cane
35½ x 15½ x 19½ in. (90.2 x 39.4 x 49.5 cm)

While close in form to chairs designed and manufactured by Michael Thonet in the last years of the 1850s (model numbers 8 and 14), details of this chair's construction and proportions indicate that it was made by an unidentified competitor of Gebrüder Thonet. Here the back legs are formed of solid wood, terminating in an inverted V approximately four inches above the seat. The back is completed by a multi-ply laminate that forms the double curve of the crest rail and backrest as did Thonet's model number 8 (the same visual effect was achieved with two separate pieces of wood screwed together in Thonet's model number 14). The circular seat is constructed from four semicircular segments of solid wood held together with wedges set into their upper surfaces. At the juncture with the front legs, the seat frame is enhanced by the addition of a wedge of wood into which the legs are doweled. The circular stretcher of three-ply laminate stabilizes the chair. In the 1850s and 1860s, native Viennese furniture makers such as Josef Neyger disputed Thonet's exclusive privileges to make furniture from bent wood. Unsuccessful in their lawsuits, they copied many of the early models introduced and made popular by Gebrüder Thonet, but used the outmoded technique of bending strips of veneer, or laminates, which Thonet's technique of bending solid lengths of wood had superseded.

9 / ARMCHAIR

Unknown manufacturer (Austrian), c. 1862
Beech, wood laminate, cane
38⅝ x 21¼ x 23 in. (98.1 x 54 x 58.4 cm)

10 / ARMCHAIR

Unknown manufacturer (Austrian), c. 1862
Beech, wood laminate, cane
38¼ x 21½ x 23 in. (97.2 x 54.6 x 58.4 cm)

Both armchairs (cat. nos. 9 and 10) attempt to solve the problem of how to attach a scrolling arm to the side chair inspired by Thonet's model numbers 8 and 14. These chairs are similar in construction to the previous side chair (cat. no. 8), being composed of solid wood as well as laminate sections. The arms of one chair (cat. no. 9) are attached low on the stiles, turning upwards and forward to finish in the scroll at the seat. This configuration, however, increases the stress in the arms, each of which is formed from two sections of eight- or nine-ply laminate spliced midway along the arm with a V-shaped joint. The armchair (cat. no. 10) shows a different resolution of the arm attachment. The multi-ply laminate arm is attached high on the shoulder of the chair and scrolls down and forward to terminate at the seat.

9 A / DETAIL OF BACK LEG-BACKREST EXTENSION, SEEN FROM BEHIND, SHOWING INTERSECTION OF SOLID WOOD AND LAMINATE

11 / SIDE CHAIR
Unknown manufacturer (Austrian), c. 1860
Beech, wood laminate, cane
39 x 16¾ x 21 in. (99.1 x 42.6 x 53.3 cm)

This chair relates to Thonet's models 7 and 12, but was produced with the non-exclusive lamination technique, in which veneer strips were soaked in glue and bent in molds to achieve their curvature. The construction of this seat can also be distinguished from models made by Gebrüder Thonet; this competitor used four segments of solid wood carved in arcs—rather than laminates or bent solid wood—to construct the seat frame.

12 / SIDE CHAIR, MODEL NO. 3
Unknown manufacturer (Austrian), c. 1860s
Beech, wood laminate, cane
36¼ x 16⅜ x 20⅜ in. (92.1 x 41.6 x 51.8 cm)

13 / SETTEE, MODEL NO. 16

Designer: Michael Thonet
(1796–1871), 1862
Manufacturer: Gebrüder Thonet
(1853–1921), after 1862
Beech, cane
51¾ x 57½ x 22⅝ in. (131.5 x 146.1 x 60 cm)

DETAIL OF BACK OF SETTEE, SHOWING WOOD FILL IN CANING CHANNELS

14 / SIDE CHAIR, MODEL NO. 16

Designer: Michael Thonet
(1796–1871), 1862
Manufacturer: Gebrüder Thonet
(1853–1921), 1862/1915
Beech, cane
45 x 18¼ x 20⅝ in. (114.3 x 46.4 x 52.4 cm)

The concept of matching sets of furniture was articulated in bent wood as early as 1851, when Thonet exhibited a side chair, armchair and settee en suite at London's Crystal Palace exhibition. This side chair and the settee of the same model (cat. no. 13) were first shown by Thonet at London's second international exhibition in 1862, where the firm offered bentwood furniture "produced at singularly small cost," in contrast to the luxury furnishings displayed in 1851. Thonet's entry in the 1862 exhibition catalog noted the recent improvements made in bentwood technology: "Whereas, formerly, the bents were consisting of several parts and glued together, now any bent whatsoever is made of one piece, hereby being adapted to every climate, which was not the case when there were glued joints."

Several variations on this model were offered through Thonet's catalogs: chair model number 17, with one elongated oval in the back (see Zelleke, fig. 4), rather than the two seen here, appears first in Thonet's broadsheet of 1866; in 1888 a suite of furniture is described as being in the "Genre gothique"—the chair backs are described by intersecting elongated oval forms surmounted by circles—to appeal to the historicist market of the late nineteenth century.

15 / ROCKING CHAIR, MODEL NO. 10
Designer: Michael Thonet (1796–1871), c. 1866
Manufacturer: Gebrüder Thonet (1853–1921), 1881/1921
Beech, cane
39½ x 21½ x 42½ in. (100.3 x 54.6 x 108 cm)

Michael Thonet's design for his first bentwood rocking chair (intended for home rather than public use) was introduced about 1860 and may have been inspired by rockers made by the Birmingham metalworker R. W. Winfield shown at London's exhibition of 1851. In the years following his first design, Thonet continued to invent new models, such as this one, in which stiles, sides of seat frames, and runners were formed of continuous lengths of bent wood, while varying the shape of the scrolling insert between the seat and the runners. The apparent delicacy of Thonet's models belied the durability of rocking chairs made with bentwood elements. While they appear to have been more popular in America than in Europe, where they were associated with invalids and children (model number 10 first appears in the firm's 1866 broadsheet catalog as a child's rocker), rocking chairs were also found in the more informal settings of European summer houses and conservatories (see Zelleke, fig. 5).

16 / RECLINING COUCH, MODEL NO. 2

Manufacturer: Gebrüder Thonet (1853–1921), after 1885
Beech, cane, iron
42½ x 25½ x 58½ in. (108 x 64.8 x 148.6 cm)

57

17 / SOFA TABLE, MODEL NO. 1
Manufacturer: Gebrüder Thonet (1853–1921), after 1885
Beech
30¾ x 31½ x 44 in. (78.1 x 80 x 111.8 cm)

Thonet's bentwood tables were first introduced in his luxury furnishings for the London exhibition of 1851. They were subsequently featured in every Thonet broadsheet catalog, the bentwood loops of the legs echoing contemporary backrest designs.

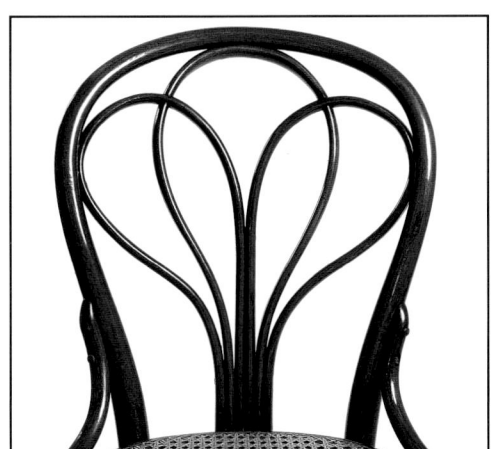

18 / SIDE CHAIR, MODEL NO. 25

Manufacturer: Gebrüder Thonet (1853–1921), c. 1883/1911 (designed c. 1875)
Beech, cane
36 x 17¼ x 21¾ in. (91.4 x 44 x 55.3 cm)

Until 1869, when their patent expired, Gebrüder Thonet had the exclusive rights to manufacture furniture from solid bentwood parts. Competition from the Viennese furniture trade, beginning in the middle of the 1850s, did not significantly challenge Thonet's technological innovations or its expansion into an international market. But by the late 1860s, would-be rivals such as the father-and-son team of Jacob and Josef Kohn were poised to enter the market for bentwood furniture on a scale that would challenge Gebrüder Thonet. The Kohn firm was not content to remain in the shadows of Thonet by reproducing its well-established models: it improved upon production methods, introduced new forms such as this chair, and experimented with the profile of bentwood rods by subtly articulating their diameters. This chair relies for its aesthetic interest not only on the manner in which the bentwood rods are interwoven, but also on the swelling and diminishing contours of the rods themselves, which give Kohn's chairs a vigor and robustness different from Thonet models of the same period.

19 / SIDE CHAIR, MODEL NO. 27

Manufacturer: Jacob & Josef Kohn (1867–1914), 1870s
Beech, cane
35¼ x 17¼ x 22 in. (89.5 x 43.8 x 55.9 cm)

59

20 / SETTEE, MODEL NO. 26
Manufacturer: Jacob & Josef Kohn (1867–1914), after 1870s
Beech, cane
39¾ x 58¼ x 23½ in. (101 x 148 x 59.7 cm)

21 / SIDE CHAIR, MODEL NO. 33

Manufacturer: Jacob & Josef Kohn (1867–1914), late 19th/early 20th century (designed 1870s)
Beech, cane
35⅜ x 18 x 24 in. (89.9 x 45.7 x 61 cm)

22 / SETTEE

Manufacturer: D. G. Fischel Söhne (1870–1938)
Beech, cane
38 x 43½ x 22 in. (96.5 x 110.5 x 55.9 cm)

Like Jacob & Josef Kohn, the firm D. G. Fischel Söhne took advantage of the expiration of Gebrüder Thonet's exclusive manufacturing privilege and entered the bentwood furniture industry in 1870. The earliest known catalog by Fischel was issued around 1890 and included bentwood classics as well as furniture with turned elements, which the firm claimed to have introduced in response to consumer demand. By 1893 they had five factories and numerous sales outlets in Europe. In 1914 and 1915 Fischel issued extensive catalogs for the international and domestic markets that included traditional bentwood pieces, such as this settee, as well as pieces influenced by architects and designers such as Josef Hoffmann and others of the artistic avant-garde of the time. This settee and the long-legged office chair (cat. no. 23) resemble models in Thonet and Kohn catalogs from the 1880s.

23 / OFFICE CHAIR

Manufacturer: D. G. Fischel Söhne (1870–1938)
Beech, cane
43½ x 18¾ x 24 in. (110.5 x 47.6 x 61 cm)

24 / SETTEE

Manufacturer: Josef Hofmann Succ. (active c. 1893)
Beech, cane
39⅜ x 55 x 27 in. (100 x 139.7 x 68.6 cm)

Rival bentwood manufacturers freely copied popular models from one another. This form was also produced by Jacob & Josef Kohn as model number 40/C. Little is known about the firm Josef Hofmann Successeurs beyond its listing in an 1893 compendium of all known bentwood furniture manufacturers.

24 A / JOSEF HOFMANN SUCC. LABEL

25 / EASY CHAIR, MODEL NO. 1

Manufacturer: Gebrüder Thonet (1853–1921), 1885/1915
Beech, cane
43½ x 25¼ x 20 in. (110.5 x 64.1 x 50.8 cm)

Thonet's financial success was due in large part to meeting the requirements of large-scale public seating: cafés, restaurants, theaters, offices, and hotels. From the late 1870s, Jacob & Josef Kohn sought to cultivate a new market for bentwood furniture—the private bourgeois home. In exhibitions in Philadelphia (1876), Paris (1878), and Antwerp (1885), Kohn displayed richly upholstered historicist furniture. Thonet also began to develop this market, offering several suites of drawing-room furniture for the first time in its twenty-six page catalog of 1885.

This example, called a "gent's easy chair," was illustrated without upholstery or cane alongside a matching settee and smaller "lady's easy chair." When covered with thick, tufted and fringed upholstery to match a particular scheme of decoration, these types of chairs could compete with the heavy, overstuffed, traditionally carved chairs in various revival styles that were fashionable in later nineteenth-century interiors (see Zelleke, fig. 6).

26 / PRIE-DIEU

Manufacturer: Gebrüder Thonet (1853–1921), 1885/1915
Beech, upholstery (new)
38 x 20¾ x 25 in. (96.5 x 52.7 x 63.5 cm)

An explosion in bentwood furniture forms occurred in the 1880s and 1890s as Thonet issued its first multi-page catalogs (1885, 1888, and 1895). Furniture was developed to meet every need—public, institutional, and private. This prayer stool, first seen in the firm's 1885 catalog, is a marvel of grace and fluidity in bent wood: each side is composed of two ribbons of wood that scroll through the entire height and depth of the stool. The pierced oval with the crucifix is poised between the arm rests and the supports. Prayer stools were part of the standard furnishings of middle- and upper-class bedrooms, ministering to mental or spiritual "hygiene" much as bentwood wash stands and mirrors (see cat. no. 27) administered to the physical.

27 / CHEVAL GLASS

Manufacturer: Gebrüder Thonet (1853–1921), 1885/1915
Beech, glass, gilt metal
77 x 43½ x 22½ in. (195.6 x 110.5 x 57.2)

28 A / LAMINATE TABLE TOP

28 / READING TABLE, MODEL NO. 1

Manufacturer: Gebrüder Thonet (1853–1921), c. 1895/1904
Beech, wood laminate
30½ x 18½ in. (77.5 x 47 cm)

This table form was first seen in Thonet's 1885 catalog; by 1895 it was available with the Renaissance-revival table top seen here. The border of the top is printed in reverse with "v. F. Lechleitner," a name that corresponds to a Viennese paper-hanging firm, which may have supplied the furniture manufacturer with patterns for transfer printing.

29 / MUSIC RACK, MODEL NO. 2

Manufacturer: Gebrüder Thonet (1853–1921), 1895/1910
Beech, wood laminate
43 x 20½ x 17½ in. (109.2 x 52.1 x 44.5 cm)

The intricate loops of bent wood that create the partitions in the rack were first seen in a shorter music stand in Thonet's 1885 catalog. Ever ready to work variations on a theme, the firm introduced this taller model in their expanded catalog of 1895. The printed lyre panel, here seen on the lower shelf of the rack, was also available for the backs of chairs, so that one could create a unified and appropriate atmosphere for the concert hall or the music room at home.

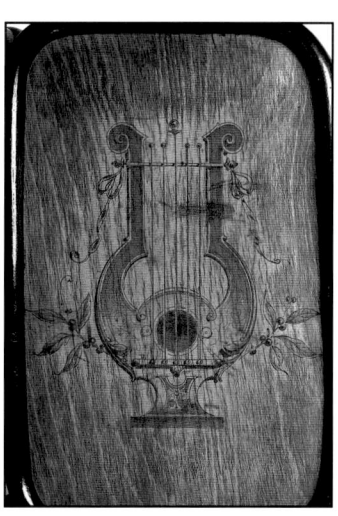

LAMINATE SHELF WITH PRINTED LYRE

GEBRÜDER THONET PAPER LABEL, IN USE FROM C. 1881 TO 1921

30 / SIDE CHAIR, MODEL NO. 51

Designer: attributed to August Thonet (1829–1910), c. 1885
Manufacturer: Gebrüder Thonet (1853–1921), c. 1900/1915
Beech, cane
36 x 16 x 20¼ in. (91.4 x 40.6 x 51.4 cm)

30 A / PAPER LABEL FOR THONET'S NEW YORK SHOWROOM AT 860 BROADWAY, IN USE FROM 1900/1901

This chair first appeared in Gebrüder Thonet's catalog of 1885 and remained in production through the firm's 1911/15 catalog along with an armchair and a stool (cat. no. 31). It exemplifies the versatility of bentwood manipulation: a single length of bentwood frames the back, extending diagonally down and forward to terminate at the front feet; another length of wood forms the hexagonal back piece and the back legs. Stability is assured by two inverted V-shaped rods that support the front corners of the seat frame and terminate at diagonally opposed front and back legs. Its design has been attributed to August Thonet, Michael's third son, who designed a number of Thonet's most technically precocious, if commercially impractical, forms for display at the many international exhibitions the firm continued to enter after Michael Thonet's death in 1871. The strongly angular note of the bent rods in this chair stands in contrast to the more curvilinear, scrolling forms of the preceding decades. This model, unlike some of August Thonet's, was designed for mass production. It was especially popular in the North American market, and was featured in Thonet's promotional photographs as seating for the dining room of New York's Hotel Astor.

31 / STOOL, MODEL NO. 51

Designer: attributed to August Thonet (1829–1910), c. 1885
Manufacturer: Gebrüder Thonet (1853–1921), 1885/1915
Beech, cane
17⅛ x 14⅞ x 14⅞ in. (43.5 x 37.6 x 37.6 cm)

32 / SIDE CHAIR, MODEL NO. 91

Designer: attributed to August Thonet (1829–1910), c. 1895
Manufacturer: Gebrüder Thonet (1853–1921), 1895/1915
Beech, cane
33 x 17 x 21¼ in. (83.8 x 43.2 x 54cm)

33 / CARD TABLE, MODEL NO. 7

Manufacturer: Gebrüder Thonet (1853–1921), 1895/1915
Beech, brass, felt (new)
30½ x 32½ x 32½ in. (77.5 x 82.6 x 82.6 cm)

34 / CHILD'S HIGH TABLE CHAIR, MODEL NO. 1

Manufacturer: Gebrüder Thonet (1853–1921), c. 1890s
Beech, wood laminate, cane, iron
36 x 19¼ x 21½ in. (91.5 x 48.9 x 54.6 cm)
Collection of Shelby Williams Industries, Inc.

As early as their 1866 broadsheet catalog, Gebrüder Thonet offered a line of bentwood furniture for children including a high chair (not this model), table, matching arm- and side chair, and a child's rocking chair (cat. no. 15 is the adult version). With each new catalog the selection expanded, so that by 1904 Thonet's offerings had grown to include carriage chairs (see cat. no. 35), combination seat and tables (see cat. no. 36), small washing stands, bedsteads, cradles (see cat. no. 37), stools, go-carts, swings, hoops and gymnasium rings, and a large selection of doll's furniture (see cat. no. 38). This model first appears in Thonet's 1885 catalog.

35 / CHILD'S CARRIAGE CHAIR, MODEL NO. 4

Manufacturer: Gebrüder Thonet (1853–1921), 1904/1915
Beech, wood laminate, cane, iron
High chair: 38½ x 19¾ x 19½ in. (97.8 x 50.2 x 49.5 cm)
Carriage: 24¾ x 19½ x 31 in. (62.9 x 49.5 x 78.7 cm)

Kohn appears to have been the first company to introduce this type of dual-purpose child's chair, a high chair that converted to a carriage, around 1877; it first appears at Thonet in the firm's 1885 catalog. This version, with its squared, rather than rounded, contours, was first offered by Thonet in 1904.

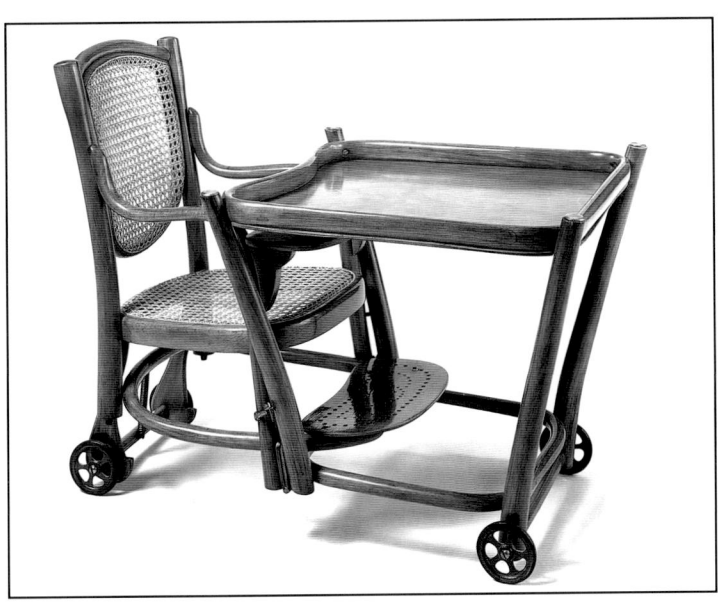

35 A / CHILD'S CARRIAGE CHAIR IN ALTERNATE POSITION

36 / CHILD'S SEAT AND TABLE
Manufacturer: Gebrüder Thonet (1853–1921), 1885/1915
Beech
22 x 18¼ x 34¼ in. (55.9 x 46.4 x 87 cm)
Collection of Shelby Williams Industries, Inc.

37 / CRADLE, MODEL NO. 1573

Manufacturer: Jacob & Josef Kohn (1867–1914), c. 1904/1916
Beech, metal
77½ x 26¾ x 53¼ in. (196.9 x 68 x 135.3 cm)

Cradles were among the new forms introduced by both Thonet and Kohn in the 1880s to appeal to the private client for home furnishings. In use, the cradle's bentwood skeleton was well padded to provide comfort for the infant. Additional material like mosquito netting or cloth would have been looped around the upright of the cradle to protect the baby from drafts.

38 / DOLL'S FURNITURE

Manufacturer: Gebrüder Thonet (1853–1921), 1885/1915
Beech, cane
Table: 9½ x 10¼ in. (24.1 x 26 cm)
Settee: 12⅝ x 14⅛ x 9¼ in. (32.1 x 35.9 x 23.5 cm)
Armchair: 12¾ x 7¾ x 9⅝ in. (32.4 x 19.7 x 24.5 cm)
Rocking chair: 11⅛ x 7¼ x 12¼ in. (28.3 x 18.4 x 31.1 cm)

39 / WOOD BASKET, MODEL NO. 2

Manufacturer: Gebrüder Thonet (1853–1921), 1885/1904
Beech, wood laminate, metal
17 x 25 x 17¼ in. (43.2 x 63.5 x 43.8 cm)

40 / ARMCHAIR FOR WRITING DESK, MODEL NO. 1

Manufacturer: Gebrüder Thonet (1853–1921), 1885/1915
Beech, wood laminate
32 1/8 x 26 5/8 x 24 in. (81.6 x 67.6 x 61 cm)

41 / MUSIC STAND, MODEL NO. 1179

Manufacturer: Jacob & Josef Kohn (1867–1914), c. 1885/1916
Beech, wood laminate
45 3/4 x 19 5/8 x 16 in. (116.2 x 49.9 x 40.6 cm)

As early as 1885, Thonet offered for sale a three-legged music stand perforated with a pattern of two lyres on the laminate board. Three years later, the firm was selling a similar stand with back-to-back racks to hold music for two musicians at once. Kohn may have begun production of its music stand at about the same time. Bentwood furniture manufacturers were untroubled by replicating a competitor's product, often copying it outright and at other times introducing variations to the design, making it difficult, in many cases, to tell where an idea originated. This music stand, with a single rack, is illustrated in Kohn's catalog of 1916 along with model number 1180, which had back-to-back racks.

42 / STAND, MODEL NO. 42
Manufacturer: Gebrüder Thonet
(1853-1921), after 1904
Beech
52 in. (132 cm)

This stand is one of the few examples of Art Nouveau–inspired furniture to appear in Gebrüder Thonet's catalog of 1904. In this model, Thonet has suspended a tray resembling a lily pad between square-sectioned rods arranged to echo the organic growth of plants. The interest in curving, asymmetrically disposed lines and forms was characteristic of the Art Nouveau, which appeared in the graphic and decorative arts of the last two decades of the nineteenth century. The style was most fully represented at the Paris Exposition Universelle of 1900, especially in the work of French and Belgian architects and designers. Of the bentwood furniture and interiors shown at the Exposition, Kohn's work was the more informed (albeit subtly) by this new taste for flowing lines and sweeping curves (see Ottillinger, fig. 11). This stand represents a rare attempt by Thonet to capture the essence of the movement. Generally, Austrian bentwood furniture of the new century took a different direction than contemporaneous French design: it used geometry, rather than the idea of organic growth, as its inspiration.

43 / BENTWOOD SPIRAL

Manufacturer: Gebrüder Thonet (1853–1921), c. 1880s
Oak
50¼ x 37½ x 3⅝ in. (127.6 x 95.3 x 9.2 cm)
Collection of Shelby Williams Industries, Inc.

Thonet's achievement was to make wood perform as a plastic material. This tour de force of bent wood, made as an exhibition piece in the 1880s, was created from a twenty-seven-foot length of oak that was steamed and bent in molds to achieve the tight scroll effect seen here.

44 / BENTWOOD SPIRAL

Manufacturer: Gebrüder Thonet (1853–1921)
Beech
37¼ in. (94.6 cm)
Collection of Shelby Williams Industries, Inc.

45 / SIDE CHAIR, MODEL NO. 255

Designer: Adolf Loos (1870–1933), c. 1898
Manufacturer: Jacob & Josef Kohn (1867–1914), 1899/c. 1906
Beech, cane
34¾ x 17¾ x 21 in. (88.3 x 45.1 x 53.3 cm)

The gentle undulations of the rods make this one of the most elegant bentwood side chairs. It was designed around 1898 by the Viennese architect Adolf Loos for the interior of the Café Museum, a fashionable Viennese coffeehouse. The first architect-designed example of bentwood furniture, this model was offered with a choice of double or triple backrest supports in Kohn's 1906 Italian-language catalog. The choice of bent wood as a material for coffeehouse furnishings had a history, going back to Thonet's model number 4 for the Café Daum in 1857 (see cat. no. 3). Style also links this chair to some of Michael Thonet's designs from the 1850s: model number 14 (see cat. no. 7) for the double arc of the back; and model number 9 (see cat no. 4) for the contour of the crest rail and the open reserves at the knees, as well as to chairs produced in the 1870s by Jacob & Josef Kohn in the swelling and diminishing profiles of the bentwood rods (see cat. no. 19). A contemporary critic, discussing the Café Museum, identified Loos's attitude to design: "Loos's starting point is the 'individuality' of the respective material . . . What does [the café] teach us? . . . it shows that simplicity and elegance come from one source: clarity."

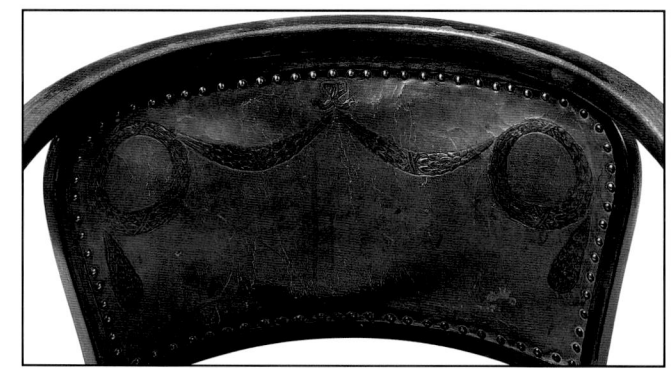

46 / ARMCHAIR, MODEL NO. 715

Designer: Gustav Siegel (1880–1970), c. 1900
Manufacturer: Jacob & Josef Kohn (1867–1914), c. 1900/1916
Beech, leather upholstery
29⁷⁄₈ x 21½ x 21¾ in. (75.9 x 54.6 x 55.3 cm)

In 1899 Gustav Siegel, a young cabinetmaker and student at the Vienna School of Applied Arts, was hired to head the design department of Jacob & Josef Kohn. Siegel presided over important changes at Kohn in the pre–World War I period as contemporary architects such as Josef Hoffmann, Koloman Moser, and Otto Wagner designed avant-garde furniture for production in bent wood. Kohn's stylish change in direction was first acclaimed at the 1900 Exposition Universelle held in Paris, where the installations Siegel designed were awarded a gold medal over those of Gebrüder Thonet. The installations not only presented bentwood furniture, but the very structure of the walls was framed and articulated with bent, square-sectioned rods. A chair closely related to this one was included in one of Siegel's interiors, differing only in the use of sabots. Three lengths of bent wood form the principal components: front legs, arm rests and crest; back legs, stiles and splat; and seat, below which three inverted U-shaped braces provide stability. The basic form of this chair was adopted by the architect Otto Wagner for the armchairs he designed for the Postal Savings Bank in Vienna between 1904 and 1906.

47 / ARMCHAIR, MODEL NO. 412

Designer: Gustav Siegel (1880–1970), c. 1902
Manufacturer: Jacob & Josef Kohn (1867–1914), 1902/1916
Beech, brass, upholstery (replacement)
32¾ x 24⅞ x 25 in. (83.2 x 63.2 x 63.5 cm)

Two years after the Paris Exposition of 1900, Kohn exhibited its self-consciously avant-garde furniture once again at the International Exhibition of Modern Decorative Art in Turin. Kohn's "Ladies' Drawing Room" included a two-tiered vitrine designed by Koloman Moser and a suite of seating furniture, attributed to Siegel, that included a settee, bench, and an armchair of this model. While related to Siegel's chair of 1900 (cat. no. 46), there are distinct differences. In the earlier chair a single rod of bent wood formed the front legs, arm rests and crest of the chair, embracing the sitter. Here the sitter is held between two bentwood braces that, as in Thonet's early "Boppard" chair (see cat. no. 2), form the legs, sides, and stiles of the chair. A particular innovation is the use of large nails at the seat and stiles, with which Siegel drew attention to the construction of the chair (just as, two years later, Otto Wagner would draw attention to the cladding of the Postal Savings Bank with prominent aluminum bolts on its facade).

48 / DESK CHAIR, MODEL NO. 721

Manufacturer: Jacob & Josef Kohn (1867–1914), c. 1902/1916
Beech, wood laminate
32 x 22⅛ x 22½ in. (81.3 x 56.2 x 57.2 cm)

49 / ARMCHAIR, MODEL NO. 330/F

Designer: Josef Hoffmann (1870–1956), c. 1901
Manufacturer: Jacob & Josef Kohn (1867–1914), 1901/1916
Beech, wood laminate, brass, upholstery
38½ x 23¼ x 24½ in. (97.8 x 59.1 x 62.2 cm)

Josef Hoffmann was one of the most influential Viennese architects and designers in the first decade of the twentieth century. From 1892 he trained under the architect Otto Wagner at the Vienna Academy of Art and later worked in Wagner's office. Hoffmann became a founding member of the Secession in 1897, espousing the equal importance of fine and decorative arts. A professor at the School of Applied Arts from 1899 and a founding member of the Wiener Werkstätte in 1903, Hoffmann helped to define the formal vocabulary of bentwood furniture in the years prior to World War I through the objects he designed for Jacob & Josef Kohn. In one of his early designs for Kohn, Hoffmann used a single rod of square-sectioned bent wood to describe the front legs, armrests and back of this chair, while a large panel of bent laminate formed the barrel back, enveloping the sitter. Brass nails with large heads secure the lower edge of the enclosure to the seat frame. The seat is covered in a contemporary textile, a pale blue ground patterned with darker blue and white circles within squares and finished by a pale golden gimp. This model was first seen as a side chair in a dining room, one of three rooms furnished by Jacob & Josef Kohn, at the 1901 Christmas exhibition at the Österreichisches Museum für Kunst und Industrie. A photograph of the installation, published in 1906 in an English journal devoted to the Austrian art revival, also showed bent wood used to define the panels beneath the chair rail and around the door frames—as Siegel had framed the walls and partitions of Kohn's installation at the Paris Exposition Universelle (see Ottillinger, fig. 11).

50 / SIDE CHAIR, MODEL NO. 322

Designer: Josef Hoffmann (1870–1956), c. 1904
Manufacturer: Jacob & Josef Kohn (1867–1914), after 1904
Beech, wood laminate, leather upholstery (replacement)
39⅜ x 17¾ x 16⅞ in. (100 x 45 x 43 cm)

In 1903 Hoffmann and Koloman Moser (1868–1918) founded the Wiener Werkstätte (Viennese Workshop), a collaborative workshop of craftsmen whose aim was "to produce good and simple articles of everyday use." Influenced by such English craft workshops as the Guild of Handicraft founded by Charles Robert Ashbee in 1888, the Wiener Werkstätte (which disbanded in 1932) was a natural outgrowth of the Secession. While the Werkstätte adopted the principle of hand craftsmanship so forcefully advocated by nineteenth-century English aestheticians and designers such as John Ruskin and William Morris, its members did not neglect the advantages that machine production afforded for the dissemination of progressive designs to a wide public. Hoffmann was actively engaged in designing furniture that could be mass-produced by commercial bentwood furniture firms.

One of the first commissions for the newly established Wiener Werkstätte was the building and furnishing of the Purkersdorf Sanatorium, a fashionable spa outside Vienna, between 1904 and 1908. This side chair was designed for use in the second-floor dining room of the Sanatorium, and later (1906) marketed by Kohn to a wider public as part of a suite including an armchair (cat. no. 51), settee, and table. A single length of bentwood forms the back legs and chair back. Two columns of circles pierce the back splat while spheres are boldly secured with large screws under the corners of the seat, at once providing decorative and structural support.

51 / ARMCHAIR, MODEL NO. 322/F

Designer: Josef Hoffmann (1870–1956), c. 1906
Manufacturer: Jacob & Josef Kohn (1867–1914), after 1906
Beech, wood laminate, leather upholstery (replacement)
39⅜ x 21⅝ x 18⅞ in. (100 x 55 x 48 cm)

52 / VITRINE, MODEL NO. 600/11

Manufacturer: Jacob & Josef Kohn (1867–1914), 1904/1916
Beech, wood laminate, glass, brass
63 x 29⅝ x 13 in. (160 x 75.3 x 33 cm)

This elegant vitrine with glass doors shows the extent to which bentwood furniture had changed since Michael Thonet made his first bentwood chair for Vienna's Café Daum (see cat. no. 3). From the beginning of the twentieth century, Kohn made a determined effort to produce contemporary pieces in a modern mode that would compete with traditionally constructed, high-style furniture in the homes, as well as the institutions, of a discriminating and style-conscious clientele.

53 / RECLINING ARM CHAIR ("SITZMASCHINE"), MODEL NO. 670

Designer: Josef Hoffmann (1870–1956), c. 1905
Manufacturer: Jacob & Josef Kohn (1867–1914), 1908/1916
Beech, wood laminate, metal
43½ x 26 x 32⅛ in. (110.5 x 66 x 81.6 cm)

Economy of parts, revealed construction, and the manipulation of geometric forms to serve both structural and decorative purposes are hallmarks of Hoffmann's expert use of wood-bending technology. In this armchair with an adjustable back (the so-called Sitzmaschine, or machine for sitting), three large bentwood loops form the back and arms and legs of the chair. The rectangular back splat is articulated by twin columns of square perforations, while spheres anchor the arms and the seat to the frame of the chair. An example of this armchair painted blue and white may have been used as a deck chair in the Purkersdorf Sanatorium; one was later exhibited by Kohn as part of a room setting at the 1908 Kunstschau (Art Show) in Vienna. Seen in a contemporary photograph (see Zelleke, fig. 11), this model was shown with thick, striped and tufted cushions on both the seat and back, adding comfort to the chair but obscuring Hoffmann's signature motif of the repeating square. In Kohn's catalog of 1916, another version of the Sitzmaschine illustrated as model no. 669 featured a fully caned back and seat.

54 / DESK

Manufacturer: Jacob & Josef Kohn (1867–1914), c. 1904
Beech, wood laminate, brass, felt (replacement)
37¾ x 43¼ x 23½ in. (95.9 x 109.9 x 59.7 cm)

55 / TWO SIDE CHAIRS, MODEL NO. 371

Designer: Josef Hoffmann (1870–1956), c. 1906
Manufacturer: Jacob & Josef Kohn (1867–1914), after 1906
Beech, wood laminate
43 x 17½ x 19½ in. (109.2 x 44.5 x 49.5 cm)

Seven spheres are poised between the tall, narrow arches of bent wood that form the backs of these uncompromisingly rigid chairs. As in Hoffmann's side chair for the Purkersdorf Sanatorium (cat. no. 50), the diameter of the rods that form the back legs and stile arches taper gradually from their widest point at the foot (for greater stability) to the smallest diameter at the crest to make the tight curve. The spheres at the juncture of the front legs and underside of the seat are also recurring motifs in Hoffmann's furniture, elements of a new twentieth-century vocabulary of ornament and design. An armchair version of this model appears in Kohn's catalog of 1906.

56 / TABLE

**Manufacturer: Jacob & Josef Kohn
(1867–1914), c. 1906**
Beech, wood laminate, brass
28½ x 23⅛ in. (72.4 x 58.7 cm)

The resemblance of this table to the side chairs of around 1906 (cat. no. 55) suggests the same designer. However, both Thonet and Kohn had their own product-design staffs, anonymous designers fluent in reworking architects' ideas and incorporating motifs into a larger range of forms. Hoffmann's chair with seven spheres suspended in its back might have inspired this table, in which similar wooden spheres are held within the four-columned central support of the table.

57 / ARMCHAIR, MODEL NO. 728

**Designer: Josef Hoffmann
(1870–1956), c. 1907
Manufacturer: Jacob & Josef Kohn
(1867–1914), 1907/1916**
Beech, wood laminate, upholstery (replacement)
29 x 21½ x 18 in. (73.7 x 54.6 x 45.7 cm)

This chair is based on one designed by Josef Hoffmann for the Cabaret Fledermaus. Supported by the Wiener Werkstätte's financial backer, Fritz Wärndorfer, this club, theater, and bar was intimately associated with the intellectual and artistic avant-garde of Vienna. Its predominantly black and white color scheme of decoration was carried into Hoffmann's chairs, painted either black or white with the spheres under the seat frame and at the top of the stiles painted in the contrasting color. The form of this chair—with the horseshoe-shaped base, the strong verticals of the back legs and stiles, and the horizontal bars in the back—was adapted in other Kohn models (see cat. no. 59).

59 / ARMCHAIR, MODEL NO. 728/3F
Manufacturer: Jacob & Josef Kohn (1867–1914), 1906/1916
Beech, wood laminate
30¼ x 22 x 19⅞ in. (76.8 x 55.9 x 50.5 cm)

Several variations of this model appear in the Kohn catalog. Model number 728/F had an upholstered seat and a rod of uniform diameter forming the continuous arm rests–crest rail. In the 1906 catalog, armchair 728/3F was part of a suite advertised as living-room furniture in the modern style.

58 / TABLE
Manufacturer: Jacob & Josef Kohn (1867–1914), c. 1916
Beech, wood laminate
29⅛ x 18⅛ x 15⅜ in. (74 x 46 x 39.1 cm)

60 / CHAIR, MODEL NO. 725

Manufacturer: Jacob & Josef Kohn
(1867–1914), c. 1902/1916
Beech, wood laminate
35¼ x 22⅝ x 23⅝ in. (89.5 x 57.5 x 60 cm)

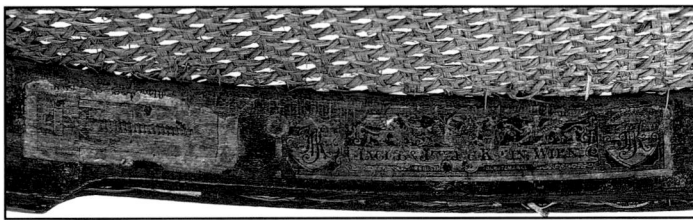

JACOB & JOSEF KOHN LABEL, IN USE C. 1902–1916

61 / TALL-CASE CLOCK, MODEL NO. 2

Manufacturer: Gebrüder Thonet (1853–1921), after 1907
Beech, wood laminate, brass, movements
79¼ x 20¼ x 12½ in. (201.3 x 51.4 x 31.8 cm)

This clock first appears in the 1907 supplement to Thonet's 1904 catalog. In this supplement, one clearly sees Thonet's response to the technological advances made by Kohn in bending square-sectioned rods at angles near ninety degrees, as well as to the modern, architect-designed furniture Kohn produced. In this clock, Thonet has managed the relatively sharp bend in the uprights as they outline the hood of the clock face.

62 / THEATER SEATING

Manufacturer: Gebrüder Thonet (1853–1921), after 1905
Beech, wood laminate, metal
37¾ x 88 x 20 in. (95.9 x 223.5 x 50.8 cm)

Social life in Vienna revolved not only around coffeehouses, but also around cabarets, musicals, and dramatic programs in the city's many theaters. Family tradition recalls that the Thonets were closely involved in this aspect of the city's cultural life, helping to found the Konzerthaus built in 1913, and to support the Volkstheater. Gebrüder Thonet saw the need for a new kind of seating in these public halls, and with its 1888 catalog sold individual chairs—and multiple seating units by 1895—in which the seats tipped up. Larger audiences could be accommodated than had been possible with over-upholstered, fixed-seat chairs, since passage in aisles was easier. The slots and circles that pierce the back panels in this unit allowed ventilation for the back as well as providing the chairs with decorative interest in the newly fashionable geometrical style. Similarly pierced panels of wood laminate are also found in the back of writing chairs that first appeared in the Thonet catalog supplement of 1905/1906.

63 / SIDE CHAIR, MODEL NO. 511

Manufacturer: Gebrüder Thonet (1853–1921), 1905/1911
Beech, wood laminate
38¾ x 16⅝ x 21⅝ in. (98.4 x 42.2 x 54.9 cm)

64 / ROCKING CHAIR, MODEL NO. 511

Manufacturer: Gebrüder Thonet (1853–1921), after 1907
Beech, wood laminate
37¼ x 21½ x 45 in. (94.6 x 54.6 x 114.3 cm)

The suite of side chair (cat. no. 63), armchair, and settee first shown in the 1905/1906 supplement to Gebrüder Thonet's 1904 catalog was enlarged by the addition of this rocking chair, which first appeared in the catalog supplement of 1907. In profile it is distinguished by the pretzel-like intersections of three arches of bent wood, the chair's armrests, stiles, and runners.

65 / TABLE, MODEL NO. 42

Manufacturer: Gebrüder Thonet
(1853–1921), after 1907
Beech, wood laminate, brass
31½ x 23 in. (80 x 58.4 cm)

**66 / UMBRELLA STAND,
MODEL NO. 9**

Manufacturer: Gebrüder Thonet
(1853–1921), 1907/1915
Beech, sheet metal, Japanese matting
35¾ x 20 x 8 in. (90.8 x 50.8 x
20.3 cm)

67 / TABLE, MODEL NO. 261

Manufacturer: Gebrüder Thonet
(1853–1921), after 1907
Beech, wood laminate, brass
28 x 16 x 16 in. (71.1 x 40.6 x 40.6 cm)

This table first appears in Gebrüder Thonet's catalog supplement of 1907, but it is related to a chair and stool (cat. nos. 30 and 31) designed around 1885 in the way pairs of bentwood rods converge at the brass-encased feet.

68 / ARMCHAIR, MODEL NO. 81

Manufacturer: Gebrüder Thonet
(1853–1921), 1907/1915
Beech, cane, iron
31⅝ x 25 x 22¾ in. (80.3 x 63.5 x 57.8 cm)

69 / SIDE CHAIR

Manufacturer: Mundus (1907–1914)
Beech, cane
34½ x 17½ x 22⅜ in. (88.6 x 44.5 x 56.8 cm)

The formal properties of this chair were not new. As early as 1873, Gebrüder Thonet offered both a chair and an armchair of this type. This Mundus example shows the enduring popularity of bentwood chair forms decades after their introduction into the market.

Leopold Pilzer (1871–1959), the driving force in the growth of the bent wood industry in the twentieth century, was born, fittingly, in the year that Michael Thonet died. At the age of sixteen, Pilzer joined Jacob & Josef Kohn; in 1893 he

MUNDUS LABEL

became a partner and guiding force in Rudolf Weill & Co., the fourth largest bentwood furniture company. Pilzer is thought to have been instrumental in waging the price wars between Austria's bent wood manufacturers in the late nineteenth and early twentieth century. In 1907, he convinced the Creditanstalt bank to finance the consolidation of sixteen smaller bentwood furniture concerns to form an effective trading bloc to compete with Thonet and Kohn. This new conglomerate was named Mundus, and, with Pilzer at the helm, aggressively pursued mergers with Kohn, incorporating it in 1914, and eight years later with Thonet AG. In 1922, the world's largest furniture corporation was formed, the holding company Mundus AG.

70 / ROCKING CHAIR, MODEL NO. 814

Manufacturer: Jacob & Josef Kohn (1867–1914), after 1904
Beech, wood laminate, metal
39½ x 21 x 36¼ in. (100.3 x 53.3 x 92.1 cm)

The flexibility of Kohn's bentwood rods can be seen in this example, in which the stiles of the rocker extend to form the double loops of the seat support and the runners on each side. The traditional form of the rocker is updated by the sharp silhouette of the flat rails alternating with stylized tree- or arrow-like shapes in the back splat. This motif was to appear on a variety of different forms produced by Kohn, including office furniture, side chairs, and a clothing stand (cat. no. 71).

71 / CLOTHING STAND, MODEL NO. 1098

Manufacturer: Kohn-Mundus (1914–1922)
Beech, wood laminate
79½ x 24½ x 24½ in. (201.9 x 62.2 x 62.2 cm)

This stark clothing rack exemplifies the good, unattributed designs that were emerging from Kohn in the first decade of the twentieth century. Square-sectioned members articulate the stand, which is boxed in at the top by four panels of wood laminate pierced with the stylized tree or arrow motif that was used on a variety of different furniture forms at this time (see cat. no. 70). While the design for this stand dates around 1906, when it appeared in Kohn's Italian-language catalog, the label on this item includes both the Mundus and Kohn trademarks, and was therefore produced sometime after the two firms merged, in 1914, and before Thonet was absorbed into the holding company, in 1922.

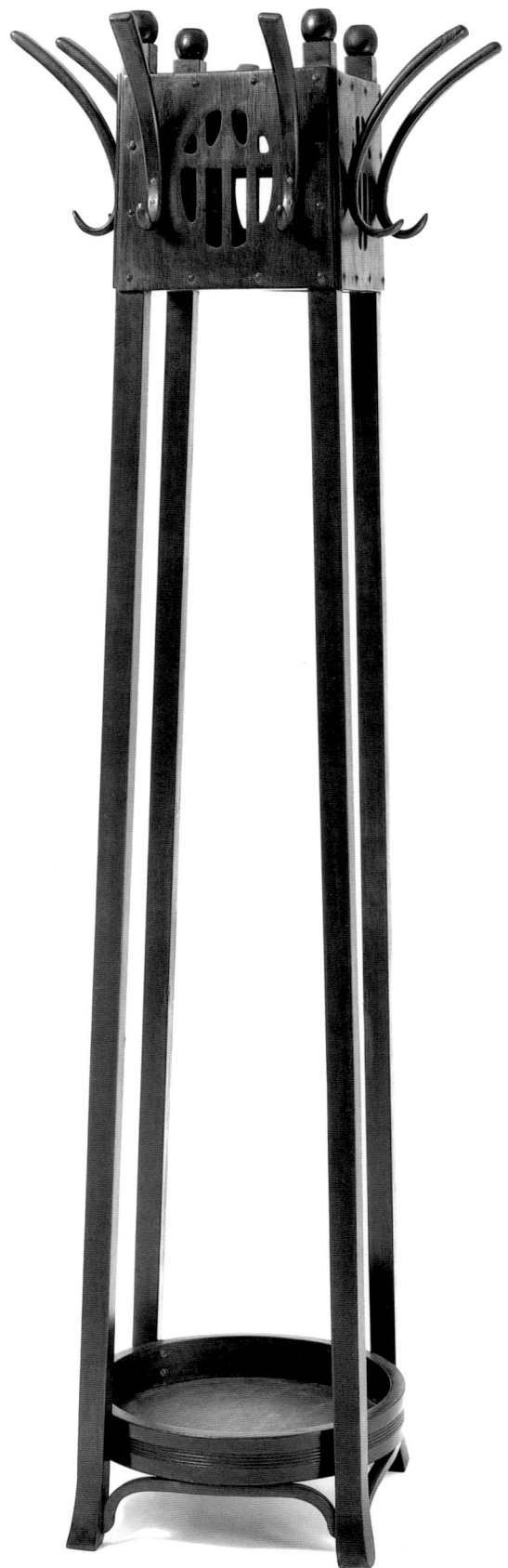

72 / SIDE CHAIR, MODEL NO. 405

Designer: Josef Urban (1872–1933), c. 1905
Manufacturer: Gebrüder Thonet (1853–1921), 1905/1911
Beech, brass, leather
38¼ x 16 x 22 in. (97.2 x 40.6 x 55.9 cm)

This chair gives little indication of its bentwood construction. Unlike Hoffmann, who used a square-sectioned rod of wood to describe the volume of his upholstered chair of about 1901 (cat. no. 49), Urban chose to emphasize the continuous sweep of leather upholstery from the chair back through seat, rather than the bentwood construction. This chair, first seen in the firm's catalog of 1905, is Urban's only securely attributed form for Gebrüder Thonet. It was pictured in contemporary photographs of domestic as well as restaurant interiors upholstered in black leather bordered with brass nails. It was later illustrated in the *Studio Year Book* of 1911 upholstered in white.

73 / HALL STAND, MODEL NO. 1369

Manufacturer: Jacob & Josef Kohn (1867-1914)/Kohn-Mundus (1914-1922), after 1916

Beech, wood laminate, mirror glass, metal

78 3/4 x 42 1/4 x 9 5/8 in. (200 x 107.3 x 24.5 cm)

Though the firm had merged with the conglomerate Mundus in 1914, Jacob & Josef Kohn issued a new catalog of designs under its own name in 1916 so as not to lose its established audience. In addition to the bentwood classics of the previous century, this catalog featured an expanded range of furniture in the spare, architectonic language of architects and designers such as Siegel and Hoffmann. Apart from the lengths of wood that form the ovals enclosing the mirror glass, there is little in this stand that technically required its manufacture in bent wood. The stark grids formed by the square-sectioned wood rods that describe this piece show the extremes to which bent wood might be taken under the geometricizing principles of early twentieth-century Viennese design. The stand has become a skeleton, almost without substance.

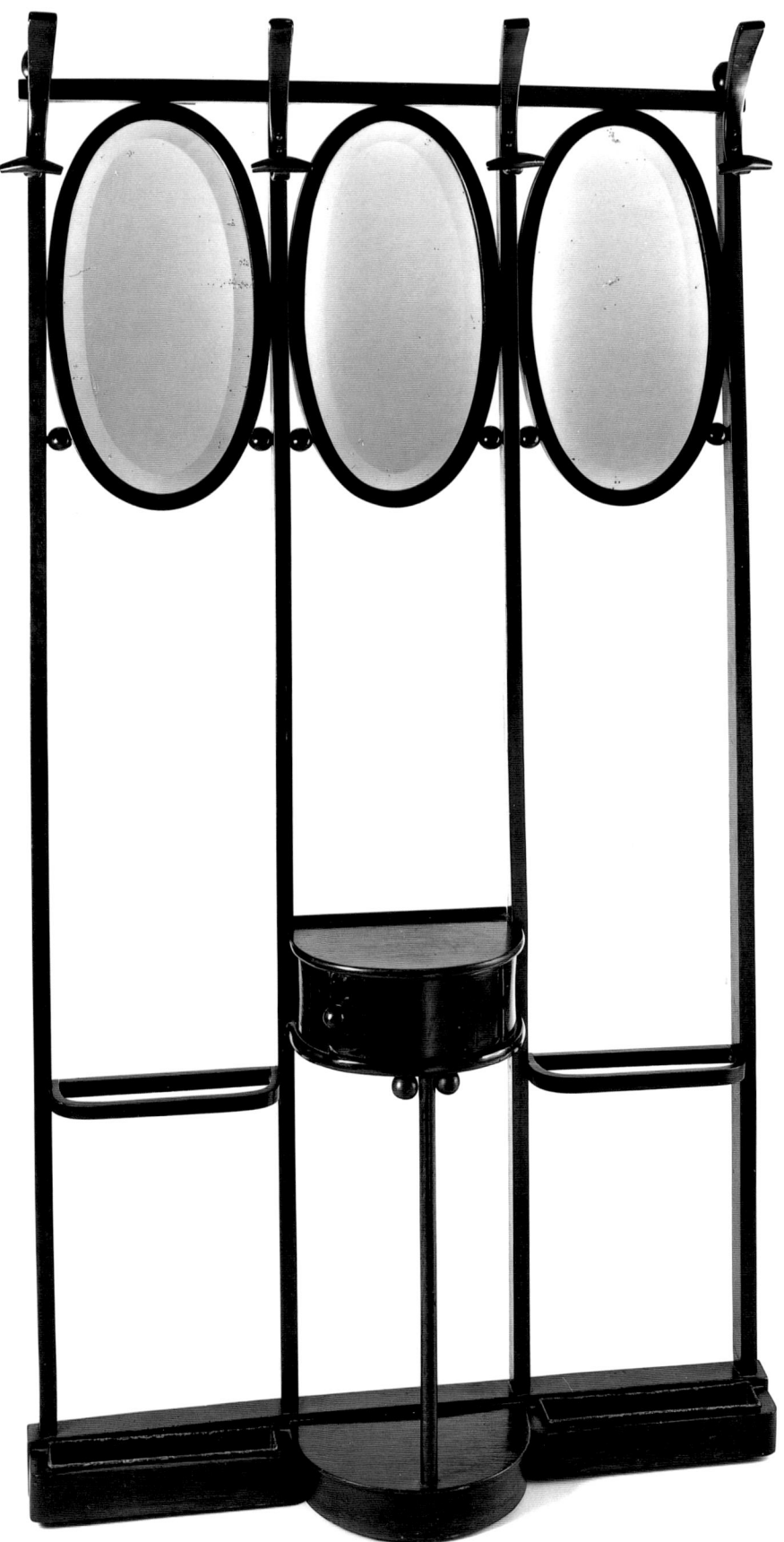

74 / SETTEE

Manufacturer: Gebrüder Thonet (1853–1921), after 1910
Beech, upholstery (replacement)
41¼ x 62 x 22½ in. (104.8 x 157.5 x 57.2 cm)

In most details this settee resembles model number 3569, illustrated in Gebrüder Thonet's catalog of about 1910, except that the oval back panels were in this case intended to be upholstered. Both settees show classically inspired details such as the fluted, pilaster-like panels that separate the three oval reserves in the back, prefiguring Art Deco designs of the 1920s. By this time, bentwood furniture had merged entirely with more traditionally crafted furniture in the stylish private interiors of the period.

THONET

MODERN FURNITURE FROM 1922 TO THE PRESENT

NINA STRITZLER

In 1936, fearing the rise of Nazism in Germany, Leopold Pilzer, director of Thonet-Mundus, transferred all his corporate assets to a Panamanian holding company, thereby maintaining financial control over the world's largest furniture manufacturer. With the conglomeration of sixteen small furniture firms, the takeover of Jacob & Josef Kohn, and finally the buyout of Gebrüder Thonet, Pilzer had smoothly navigated a series of corporate mergers that consolidated a bentwood furniture empire. Michael Thonet's skill as a craftsman led to a revolution in the design and production of bentwood furniture in the nineteenth century; Pilzer's business acumen led to a revolution in the structure of the industry. This essay traces the history of the Thonet company from 1922 until the present time.

By exploiting the profound economic and political crisis in Germany during and after World War I and in masterminding the unification of Europe's three largest bentwood furniture manufacturers, Leopold Pilzer became one of the twentieth century's first corporate raiders. In 1914 Pilzer merged his own company, Mundus, with the financially weakened Jacob & Josef Kohn, and in 1918 he moved Kohn-Mundus to Switzerland, where it was protected from the economic upheaval of World War I. Financial setbacks forced the conversion of Gebrüder Thonet to a public stock company in 1921, and by 1922 it was obliged to relinquish control to Pilzer, who then exchanged his shares to the holding company Mundus Allgemeine Handels- und Industrie Gessellschaft.[1] The Thonet family retained a small percentage of the company, but all of the bent wood factories in Europe were henceforth under Pilzer's direction. Pilzer orchestrated Thonet's rapid recovery after World War I and secured his control by placing his two stepsons in key company positions. John L.

Weill became head of Thonet operations in Austria, and Bruno Weill became director of Thonet Frères, Paris. By 1925 Thonet was again producing bentwood furniture for the worldwide market.

Thonet's renewal after the war was initially facilitated by the appeal of bentwood furniture to a broad clientele, including commercial and mainstream consumers as well as to leading exponents of the burgeoning Modern Movement. Thonet maintained an important export business during the interwar years. A plant in New York City, for example, assembled bentwood furniture prepared in Eastern Europe to be sold in the United States. American Thonet catalogs from the 1920s were quite conservative,[2] offering many designs inspired by Sheraton, Hepplewhite, and other traditional forms. These types of chairs were particularly attractive to American customers who purchased bent wood primarily for its strength and durability. The low cost was also an important sales factor and contributed to the widespread use of bentwood furniture in commercial locations. Advantageous buys were offered for large orders, and costs decreased with purchases made by the dozen.

The ubiquity of bentwood furniture in Modern Movement interiors reflected the radical changes occuring in architecture and design during the 1920s. Of the numerous models produced by Thonet, a select few, including model numbers 9 (cat. no. 4) and 18, were revered by Modern architects. These examples embodied the ideas of mass production, economy, and the harmonious integration of structure and decoration. This last feature in particular complied with the reductivist approach of the Modernist designers.

The history of Thonet's association with the Modern Movement generally begins with Le Corbusier, who is credited with initiating the bent wood revival among adherents of the "new architecture."[3] The first public manifestation of bentwood furniture in a Corbusian interior occurred in the Esprit Nouveau pavilion at the 1925 Exposition of Modern Decorative and Industrial Arts. The pavilion interior and furnishings were integral to Le Corbusier's program for "equipement de l'habitation," a classification system that categorized the domestic interior by function. The model number 9 chair was featured there as a signifier of mass-production types, the antithesis of the traditional French notion of luxury, one-of-a-kind handcrafted furniture. Formal concerns contributed to the design of the pavilion as a *Gesamtkunstwerk*, a total work of art. Nancy Troy has argued that the design must be situated in relation to Purist painting: an emphatic geometric order and the rendering of objects to disclose their hidden structure related the morphology of model number 9 to Purism's dictates.[4] Thus the selection of the "humble" Thonet chair as a Modern icon must be understood within the context of how both industry and art informed design.

In Germany, Thonet's success among leading exponents of the Modern Movement was more far-reaching, and was inextricable from the discourse on low-income housing, which intensified after World War I and resulted in discussions of "reforming" interiors and furnishings.[5] The activities of the German Werkbund contributed significantly to Thonet's reception in German avant-garde circles. Established in 1907 with the goal of enhancing German design productivity by creating alliances between artist, craftsman, and industry, the Werkbund was a major proponent of design reform, and throughout the interwar years played a critical role in promoting modern design through public exhibitions.[6] During the 1920s the Werkbund began to collaborate with the architects of the Neues Bauen, an organization of progressive architects devoted to the issue of mass-constructed public housing, and in 1927 the Stuttgart branch of the Werkbund sponsored the "Siedlung" (settlement) exhibition, a housing development intended to manifest the hegemony of the Modern Movement. Under the direction of Ludwig Mies van der Rohe, sixteen of the foremost architects of the Modern Movement were selected to design dwellings on Stuttgart's Weissenhof hillside. The housing exhibition was accompanied by other displays, located in an adjacent area, devoted to modern design and industry. The 1927 "Siedlung" has been described as a "landmark" and a "triumph" for Thonet:

> never before in the twentieth century had so many Thonet chairs been seen at an international exhibition. The association of Thonet furniture with the new architecture was established or reinforced, in the mind of the design community....Of the sixteen architects who designed one or more of the thirty-three housing units, one-half used Thonet bentwood chairs. Of the mass-produced furniture...an even higher percentage was made by Thonet.[7]

The prevalence of bentwood chairs was informed by the notion of *typenmöbel*, standardized "type-forms," which had been part of the Werkbund discourse on reform furniture since before the war.

The climate of reform stimulated Thonet's expansion of the bentwood line and its development of architect-designed models. Among those who created designs for Thonet were Adolf Schneck and Ferdinand Kramer, both of whom became important spokesmen for modern design.[8] Thonet did not alter its marketing practices, however, and the designers of bentwood furniture were not credited in the catalogs.

The height of Thonet's success as an innovator came in the late 1920s, when the company became the world's leader in the production of tubular-steel furniture. The inherent qualities of tubular steel—its light weight, transparency, and most particularly its structural resiliency—appealed to the Modernists. Tubular steel seemed devoid of any vestige of the past, and carried strong associations with the machine. The prominence of tubular-steel furniture at the 1927 "Siedlung" is thought to have been the impetus behind Thonet's entry into the market.[9] Beginning in 1928 Thonet produced tubular-steel designs by Marcel Breuer (see fig. 1), who designed the first tubular-steel chair at the Bauhaus in 1925, and in 1929 it purchased Standard-Möbel, Breuer's own tubular-steel furniture company.[10]

FIGURE 1

Armchair B3 (called "Wassily"), 1927/28

Designed by Marcel Breuer

Produced by Thonet

Chrome-plated tubular steel and canvas

Collection of the Museum of Modern Art, New York. Gift of Herbert Bayer

FIGURE 2

Armchair called "Fauteuil Basculant," 1929

Designed by Le Corbusier, Charlotte Perriand, and Pierre Jeanneret

Produced by Thonet

Chrome-plated tubular steel and canvas

Collection of the Museum of Modern Art, New York. Gift of Thonet Brothers, Inc.

FIGURE 3
Cover page, Thonet Frères, Paris, catalog of designs by Le Corbusier, Pierre Jeanneret, and Charlotte Perriand, c. 1930

Courtesy of Thonet Industries

Tubular-steel furniture was marketed separately from bent wood, and Thonet's first catalog, published in 1929, was largely composed of Breuer's designs. Thonet aggressively pursued this revolutionary market and moved to position itself as the world's undisputed leader in the production of tubular-steel furniture. In 1928, the firm acquired the license to manufacture three chairs by the design team of Le Corbusier, Charlotte Perriand, and Pierre Jeanneret.[11] The "Fauteuil Basculant" (see fig. 2), Grand Comfort, and Chaise Lounge were displayed at the 1929 Salon d'Automne in Paris, and Thonet had produced as well the metal storage cabinets in the installation.[12] As the world's largest producer of furniture, Thonet was logistically positioned to manufacture these significant new designs; as its commitment to tubular steel expanded, Thonet increased its tubular steel sales and publicity campaign in France.

The Thonet office in Paris published a new type of "loose-page" catalog composed of sixty-four designs, most of them by Breuer. It included the B3, B5, B11, and B9 chairs (see appendix, nos. 61, 62) that Breuer had produced while he was at the Bauhaus. Although the manufacture of tubular-steel furniture was clearly a dramatic departure for Thonet, its production and distribution conformed to many of the expedient bent wood production methods. This was particularly the case with Breuer's chairs, which were "uncomplicated designs manufactured from a minimum of bent steel parts" and could be "shipped knocked down."[13] The cost of steel exceeded that of bent wood, but Thonet was able to lower the price of chairs, notably Breuer's. The designs by Le Corbusier, Perriand, and Jeanneret involved more complex welding techniques, and were far more expensive to produce.

Thonet adopted a strategy for marketing tubular-steel furniture of indicating the designer's name in the sales catalog. While licensing agreements likely played a significant part in ensuring the identification of the designer, names became an important marketing tool as well. This was the beginning of "signature" furniture designs in the twentieth century. In fact, the chairs designed by Le Corbusier, Perriand, and Jeanneret were published for the French market in a separate catalog (see fig. 3) with the designers' names on the cover.[14] Ostensibly Le Corbusier's name had by that time become an effective sales device.

The most significant tubular-steel furniture design produced during the late 1920s was the cantilever chair.[15] Mart Stam produced the first model of this type, a rather awkward cantilever form lacking the resilience and refinement subsequently achieved by Breuer and Mies. In 1929 Thonet began producing Breuer's cantilever chair, model B33, without securing patent rights. A suit filed by Anton Lorenz, who had acquired the rights to these designs from Mart Stam, engaged Thonet in a complex dispute over the authorship of the cantilever chair. The court ruling awarded an artistic patent right to Mart Stam, forcing Thonet to pay royalties to Lorenz on cantilever design products. Subsequent to this ruling Thonet acquired Lorenz's company, Desta Möbel.

The tubular-steel furniture designed by Mies van der Rohe was first made at the Berliner Metallgewerbe Joseph Muller, and beginning in 1931 by Thonet.[16] Thonet produced Mies's designs for seating furniture and tables as well as a steel bed attributed to his associate Lily Reich.[17] Mies is thought to have devised the MR designation for his furniture that was subsequently adopted by Thonet. The cantilever models he designed were marketed as the MR 533 side chair and the MR 534 armchair (fig. 4). Thonet's 1932 catalog introduced the cantilever designs as lounge chairs, MR 543 and MR 544. Although Mies's first cantilever designs derived from Mart Stam's original cantilever form, they reveal the unsurpassed elegance and simplicity that Mies achieved with this

FIGURE 4
Armchair MR 534, c. 1931
Designed by Ludwig Mies van der Rohe
Produced by Thonet
Tubular steel and canvas
Collection of the Museum of Modern Art, New York.
Gift of Edgar Kaufmann, Jr.

medium. Mies's rather unusual contract with Thonet indicated that he was to be paid an annual retainer in addition to income he received from royalties.[18] Royalty figures were recorded by Thonet through 1943, an indication that tubular-steel furniture was manufactured by Thonet during World War II.[19]

Thonet was the undisputed leader in the production of tubular-steel furniture by the 1930s. The company was represented at prominent international forums such as the 1930 German Werkbund exhibit at the Paris Salon des Artistes Décorateurs (see fig. 5), the first public manifestation of German design in France since the outbreak of World War I, and in Tokyo, at the New German Architectural Arts exhibition intended to promote cultural exchange between the two countries.[20] By the early 1930s Thonet was exporting tubular-steel furniture internationally, and it distributed catalogs to England, the United States, and Scandinavia. Thonet Frères also expanded its tubular-steel line and engaged new designers, including A. Guyot and Emile Guillot (see appendix, no. 66). This furniture, however, lacked the formal rigor evinced in designs by exponents of the Modern Movement, softening the appearance of the steel structure. One chair, for example, attributed in the catalog to R. C. Coquery, revealed little of its support frame, emphasizing the fully upholstered leather seat and back.[21] But the popularity of tubular steel in France was evident by its reception among members of the newly formed Union des Artistes Modernes and by the French press.[22]

In the early 1930s, when the popularity of tubular-steel furniture was at its height, production was curtailed due to the Depression and the rise of National Socialism in Germany. As a Jewish industrialist, Pilzer was likely to have been an early target of anti-Semitic attacks, and by 1932 had the foresight to begin moving the Thonet interests to the United States.[23] Devising a strategy that would secure his assets, Pilzer transferred his Mundus AG capital stock to a Panamanian holding company.[24] In 1939, after the annexation of Austria, the German and Austrian factories were transferred back to the Thonet family. Pilzer retained control of the company branches in France, England, and the United States, as well as of the trademark and the Eastern European factories. He emigrated to the United States from Switzerland in 1940. The holding company Mundus AG became Thonet Industries, Inc., in 1945.

The German company Gebrüder Thonet, based in Frankenberg, today is still owned and operated by members of the family, George Thonet (the great-grandson of Michael Thonet) and his sons Claus, Philipp, and Peter. Thonet Vienna is owned by great-great-grandchildren of the founder, Evamarie Schmertzing-Thonet and Richard Thonet. The Eastern European factories were nationalized by their respective governments after World War II, and are now undergoing privatization. Thonet Industries, Inc., sold Thonet Frères of France to its management in 1962; the French company primarily distributes "classic" bentwood models produced in the former Thonet and Kohn factories in Eastern Europe. The European and American companies that bear the Thonet name are all independent, though discussions are currently underway to form an international marketing program.

While Thonet had maintained a large American distribution of bentwood furniture during the interwar years, its facilities were limited to storage and assembly plants, and showrooms in New York City. Eugene Halward, who had been affiliated with Thonet in Prague, preceded Pilzer in coming to the United States and was responsible for finding a suitable location and equipping a factory for the production of bentwood furniture. Statesville, North Carolina, strategically situated in a manufacturing region, was selected as the factory site. By 1943 Pilzer had purchased two other factories that he placed under the direction of his two stepsons. John L. Weill took control of the well-established American Chair Company, in Sheboygan, Wisconsin, known for producing traditional furniture for the commercial market, and Bruno Weill became the director of the York,

FIGURE 5
Deutscher Werkbund installation, Paris Salon des Artistes Decorateurs, 1930
Courtesy of Thonet Industries

Pennsylvania, factory formerly known as the Home Furniture Company. The York plant was devoted to the production of case goods and bent plywood furniture. These three factories established Thonet as a major manufacturer in America.[25]

When Thonet moved to the United States in the early 1940s, the American furniture industry was in a period of rapid change and transition. During the 1920s America had lagged behind Europe in the development of innovative furniture, and continuing through the early 1930s the major design achievements came from abroad. The Finnish architect Alvar Aalto's revolutionary laminated plywood furniture, for example, was imported to the United States and displayed in a New York showroom.[26] America's position began to change with the advent of the industrial designer. Initially, in the period after the Depression, the industrial designer focused on packaging, working to stimulate market demand by enhancing consumer appeal through superficial styling. This new influence became more decisive when manufacturers engaged industrial designers in product development to exploit new materials and technologies. Among the pioneers of the industrial design profession were Norman Bel Geddes, Raymond Loewy, and Henry Dreyfuss.

America did have its own furniture design innovators. Charles Eames and Eero Saarinen were recognized as important design leaders in 1941 when their molded plywood chairs were displayed at the Museum of Modern Art exhibition "Organic Design for Modern Living."[27] Eames and Saarinen were exceptions, however, and American furniture companies remained remarkably conservative. The industry was apparently slow to keep up with the American designer, and a schism existed between experiments in new technologies and manufacturers unwilling to invest in retooling factories to meet new production demands. In 1947, the acclaimed designer George Nelson published his famous attack on the American furniture industry, criticizing its reliance on century-old prototypes and antiquated means of production.[28]

Thonet took a conservative approach to the American market after World War II and directed its products to the contract market, supplying furniture for large commercial and institutional projects. Its staple product continued to be bentwood furniture, and it often used traditional designs to reinforce its reputation for quality production. It did invest in state-of-the-art equipment and was one of the first American furniture companies with electronic laminating facilities (see fig. 6). "Bentply" was the trademark for Thonet's new American line of plywood furniture produced from electronically molded and pressed veneers.[29] Aalto and Eames had revolutionized plywood furniture, which Thonet had actually produced in the nineteenth century.

Between 1944 and 1945 Thonet received four Bentply patents awarded for innovative joinery and upholstery, not for new developments in overall design. Most of the Bentply line derived from Aalto and Eames furniture. Bentply model number 1298 was included in a Walker Art Center exhibition of plywood furniture in its Everyday Art Gallery in September 1946.[30] Three of the early Bentply models (numbers 1216, 1294 and 1298; see fig. 7) are still in production. During the 1940s, another popular, Aalto-inspired model was introduced, a small stool with a molded plastic seat and plywood legs. Thonet purchased the plastic seats from a distributor and joined them to bent plywood legs.

During a period when Knoll Associates and Herman Miller were dramatically changing the American furniture industry by working with many outside designers, Thonet relied heavily on its in-house staff, who addressed the needs of a conservative clientele more interested in durability than innovation. Thonet's relationships with outside designers were usually not based on a long-term

FIGURE 6
Electronic molding machine at the Statesville, N.C., plant of Thonet Industries

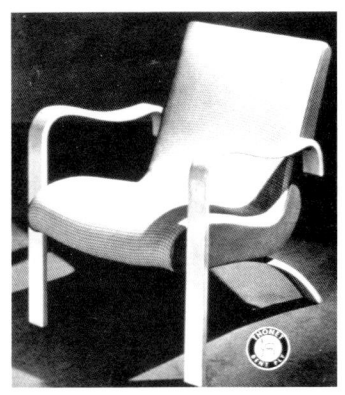

FIGURE 7
Armchair, model number 1288, c. 1945
Plywood
Produced by Thonet Industries
Courtesy of Joan M. Burgasser

FIGURE 8
Exhibition commemorating the hundredth anniversary of the founding of Gebrüder Thonet, 1953, Museum of Modern Art, New York.
Courtesy of Thonet Industries

commitment.[31] The Finnish designer Ilmari Tapiovaara produced two notable designs for Thonet: a Bentply lounge chair that was featured at the Museum of Modern Art's "Low-Cost Furniture" exhibition in 1947 but never went into production, and a metal and plywood stacking chair. Walter Gropius designed a Bentply captain's chair, an updated version of the traditional model produced at the American Chair Company. Two notable in-house designers who worked with Bentply during the 1950s were Joe Adkinson and Jean Giacomini. In 1953, Thonet's one-hundred year anniversary of sales in America was celebrated by an exhibition at the Museum of Modern Art (see fig. 8) organized by Greta Daniel.[32] Adkinson produced a commemorative chair for the exhibition, model number 1368, that was conceived as a sectional seating unit. In the centenary year, Thonet also opened a showroom in Los Angeles, its first on the West Coast.

Thonet's most important commissions of the 1950s, however, relied on outsiders. Abel Sorenson designed a molded plywood armchair, model number 1032, for the United Nations General Assembly (see fig. 9), and Walter Dorwin Teague created lounge chairs and tables of anodized aluminum for the officer's club at the United States Air Force Academy in Colorado Springs. Teague's design conformed to the corporate style then promoted by Knoll Associates.

Thonet introduced in the late 1970s a line of injection-molded polypropylene furniture designed by Gerd Lange in the 1960s and produced by Gebrüder Thonet of Frankenberg. Although these designs, marketed under the name Flex, were quite popular in Europe, they failed to gain acceptance in the United States.[33] Thonet's success continued to be in bentwood, plywood, and metal furniture. Its dependence on nineteenth-century bentwood designs was underscored when the company moved to expanded quarters at its Park Avenue location in the early 1960s: an extensive area was devoted to a "museum" of historic bentwood pieces that would be seen by clients as they entered the showroom.

The death of Leopold Pilzer in 1959 precipitated profound changes in the company's structure. Pilzer was succeeded by Bruno Weill, who was president until his death in 1962. John Weill remained with Thonet for four years after it was purchased by Simmons Corporation in 1962. In 1979 Simmons was acquired by Gulf and Western Corporation.[34] Ownership changed hands once again in 1987, when Thonet Industries, Inc., became a division of Shelby Williams Industries, Inc. This period of instability in the corporate structure of the company, an augury of the mergers now common in the furniture industry, actually stimulated important changes in Thonet's design program.

In the early 1970s, Thonet shifted away from in-house designers to an almost exclusive use of independent designers and introduced a research program for development of new materials and technology.[35] During this period of rejuvenation, a number of significant designs were introduced, including David Rowland's Sof-Tech Chair, a tubular-steel support frame with a seat and back of vinyl-coated springs that gave the chair enhanced resiliency (see appendix, no. 74). Rowland's design, now executed in six different versions, received the International Business Designer's award in 1979. More up-to-date chairs of molded plywood were also put into production. Don Petitt began working with Thonet in 1978. His Petitt Chair, the first in a series of plywood designs currently in the Petitt Ply Collection, is an elegant design in which a slender plywood frame supports a plastic shell upholstered in molded foam. Thonet also modernized its health-care line by introducing Joe Russo and Rick Sonder's "Kangaroo" chair in 1979 (see appendix, no. 75). One of the more adventurous models never put into production was designed by Peter Danko in 1980, a chair executed from a single sheet of plywood formed in a specially designed mold.

At the 1981 Chicago NEOCON, Thonet commissioned the architects Thomas Beeby, Helmut Jahn, Ronald Krieck, Kenneth Schroeder, and Stanley Tigerman to redesign its showroom in commemoration of the company's 150th anniversary. The "Thonet Takes 5" project asserted the interaction between architecture and the history of Thonet bentwood furniture, and was part of a "rethink Thonet" campaign devised to refine and modernize the Thonet image.

In the late 1980s, after the acquisition by Shelby Williams, Thonet reissued some of the classic tubular-steel and bent-plywood models, sometimes making slight alterations to the original specifications. Thonet introduced an innovative health-care chair designed by John Caldwell, who also designed the Main Frame series, featuring a unique method of quickly replacing the exterior covers, in 1992. The Attiva Collection by Jerome Caruso received the Silver Medal Award from the Industrial Designer's Society of America (see appendix, no. 79). Among the internationally recognized designers whose models Thonet is currently producing are Just Bernhard Meijer, Christina and Lars Anderson, and Studio Diemme of Italy.[36]

The advent of Modernism during the interwar years was an important catalyst for Thonet's evolution as a pioneer of furniture design in the twentieth century. The revival of bentwood furniture and the development of tubular steel became a hallmark of modern interiors. Leopold Pilzer understood the implications of Modernism on furniture production and responded quickly to take control of the new market. The number of progressive architects contracted by Thonet during the late 1920s and 1930s was unprecedented. After Thonet's move to the United States, it became a more hesitant innovator. Today Thonet pledges to uphold the commitment to design development revived during the 1970s. The bentwood and tubular-steel "classics" remain essential to this effort.

FIGURE 9
United Nations General Assembly room with bent plywood chairs by Thonet Industries
Courtesy of Thonet Industries

NOTES

1. See Christopher Wilk, *Thonet: 150 Years of Furniture* (Woodbury, N.Y., 1980), pp. 77–78.

2. A selection of such catalogs is available in the archives of the Department of Architecture and Design at the Museum of Modern Art, New York.

3. See Wilk (note 1), pp. 84–86; and *Le Corbusier: Architect of the Century*, exh. cat. Arts Council of Great Britain, London (1987), p. 212.

4. See Nancy J. Troy, *Modernism and the Decorative Arts in France: Art Nouveau to Le Corbusier* (New Haven, Conn., 1991), ch. 4.

5. For a detailed account of the reform movement, see Richard Pommer and Christian F. Otto, *Weissenhof 1927 and the Modern Movement in Architecture* (Chicago, 1991).

6. Ibid.

7. Wilk (note 1), p. 86.

8. Ibid., p. 88.

9. Ibid., p. 98.

10. Ibid., pp. 99–100.

11. Ibid., pp. 103–05.

12. Leon Deshairs, "Le Mobilier et les Arts Decoratifs au Salon d'Automne," *Art et Decoration* (December 1929), pp. 171–92.

13. See Wilk (note 1), pp. 99–100.

14. According to Wilk (note 1), the furniture appeared in the 1928 "loose page" catalog with Breuer's. The catalog noted here was a small fold-out version devoted solely to their designs.

15. See Wilk (note 1), p. 102.

16. See Ludwig Glaeser, *Ludwig Mies van der Rohe: Furniture and Furniture Drawings from the Design Collection and the Mies van der Rohe Archive* (New York, 1977).

17. Ibid., p. 14.

18. The original contract and documents pertaining to royalties are located in the Mies van der Rohe Archive, Museum of Modern Art, New York, folders 8.1 and 9.0–9.9.

19. These figures are included in the Mies van der Rohe Archive (note 18), folder 9. In 1941 Thonet listed production figures from Frankenberg, Dusseldorf, Berlin, and Hamburg amounting to 215,988.82 reichmarks. In 1943 the amount was 45,582.05 reichmarks.

20. For an account of this exhibition, see Akio Izutsu, *The Bauhaus: A Japanese Perspective* (Tokyo, 1981).

21. See Wilk (note 1), pp. 108–11.

22. See *Les Annees UAM, 1929–1958*, exh. cat. Musée des Arts Decoratifs, Paris (1988).

23. Jeffry Herf, in *Reactionary Modernism: Technology, Culture and Politics in Weimar and the Third Reich* (Cambridge, Mass., 1984) provides an account of anti-Semitism directed at Jewish industrialists.

24. This might have been arranged through a Parisian firm that specialized in creating holding companies in Panama.

25. Guido Baumgartner, who worked for Thonet beginning in the mid-1950s, provided information on the different factories in an interview with the author.

26. Aalto furniture was imported to the United States through Finmar and Artek Pascoe. Advertisements for Aalto furniture appeared regularly in *Interiors*.

27. See Martin Eidelberg, ed., *Design 1935–1965: What Modern Was*, exh. cat. Le Musée des Arts Decoratifs de Montréal (New York, 1991).

28. George Nelson, "The Furniture Industry," *Fortune* (January 1947), pp. 106–11, 171–74.

29. See Wilk (note 1), pp. 125–27.

30. The chair was illustrated in an installation photograph of the Walker Art Center exhibition in *Interiors* (September 1946). Gebrüder Thonet, which is not discussed in this essay, produced more innovative designs after the factories were rebuilt. Its production is discussed in Wilk (note 1).

31. Many of its outside designers had previously worked for Knoll.

32. No catalog was published with this exhibition.

33. The plastic chairs were inspired by Italian designs, particularly examples by Joe Colombo.

34. See Wilk (note 1), p. 131.

35. Joan Burgasser, who was associated with Thonet Industries as vice-president of design, provided an interview with the author and information on design changes in the period 1962–86, and made available catalogs and photographs.

36. The German Gebrüder Thonet, which initially aimed its classic bentwood and Bauhaus-period models at households, evolved in the 1970s as a leader of contemporary-style products for the contract market. It retains the internationally known designers Gerd Lange, Hartmuth Lohmeyer, Ulrich Bohme, and Wolf Schneider. Thonet Vienna continues to produce Hoffmann, Wagner, and Siegel designs of the Secession period. In the early 1980s it reintroduced the 1935 Art Deco designs of Marcel Kammerer. Ernest W. Beranek created the Fine Forms Collection of contemporary products.

APPENDIX

OTHER FURNITURE FROM THE STEINFELD COLLECTION

1 / SIDE CHAIR, MODEL NO. 2
Designer: Michael Thonet, c. 1854
Manufacturer: Gebrüder Thonet, after 1854
Beech, cane
37 x 16½ x 21¼ in.

2 / ARMCHAIR, MODEL NO. 3
Designer: Michael Thonet, c. 1854
Manufacturer: Gebrüder Thonet, after 1854
Beech, cane
37 x 21 x 23 in.

3 / ARMCHAIR, MODEL NO. 14
Designer: Michael Thonet, 1857/1858
Manufacturer: Gebrüder Thonet, c.1881/1921
Beech, cane
37½ x 21 x 25¾ in.

4 / SETTEE, MODEL NO. 2
Designer: Michael Thonet, c. 1859
Manufacturer: Gebrüder Thonet, c.1862/1881
Beech, cane
37½ x 45 x 25½ in.

5 / FOLDING CHAIR, MODEL NO. 1
Manufacturer: Gebrüder Thonet, after 1866
Beech, cane, upholstery
35⅛ x 18¼ x 29⅛ in.
Collection of Shelby Williams Industries, Inc.

6 / ROCKING CHAIR, MODEL NO. 7
Manufacturer: Gebrüder Thonet, after 1885
Beech, cane
30½ x 20½ x 32½ in.

7 / CHILD'S ROCKING CHAIR, MODEL NO. 7
Manufacturer: Gebrüder Thonet, after 1885
Beech, cane
25¼ x 15¾ x 26 in.
Collection of Shelby Williams Industries, Inc.

8 / ROCKING CHAIR, MODEL NO. 11
Manufacturer: Gebrüder Thonet, after 1885
Beech, cane
40¼ x 22⁷⁄₁₆ x 42 in.

9 / SIDE CHAIR, MODEL NO. 31
Manufacturer: Gebrüder Thonet,
after 1885
Beech, wood laminate
33⅞ x 17⅜ x 21½ in.

10 / FLOWER TABLE, MODEL NO. 3
Manufacturer: Gebrüder Thonet,
after 1885
Beech, wood laminate
32⅛ x 22 in.

11 / SCREEN, MODEL NO. 1
Manufacturer: Gebrüder Thonet,
after 1885
Beech
48½ x 35⅜ x 16 in.

12 / TOWEL RAIL, MODEL NO. 1
Manufacturer: Gebrüder Thonet,
after 1885
Beech
35¼ x 27⅜ x 12½ in.

13 / WALKING STICK/CHAIR
Manufacturer: Gebrüder Thonet,
after 1885
Beech, cane, metal
29¼ x 8¾ in.

14 / READING TABLE, MODEL NO. 1
Manufacturer: Gebrüder Thonet,
after 1888
Beech
30½ x 18¾ in.

15 / SIDE CHAIR, MODEL NO. 26
Manufacturer: Jacob & Josef Kohn,
after 1881
Beech, cane
35⅜ x 17 x 23¼ in.

16 / ARMCHAIR, MODEL NO. 35
Manufacturer: Jacob & Josef Kohn,
after 1881
Beech, cane
34¼ x 21 x 23⅞ in.
Collection of Shelby Williams
Industries, Inc.

17 / SETTEE, MODEL NO. 33

Manufacturer: Jacob & Josef Kohn, after 1880s

Beech, cane

41½ x 56½ x 26¾ in.

18 / SIDE CHAIR

Manufacturer: Josef Hofmann Succ., c. 1893

Beech, cane

34¼ x 16 x 17 in.

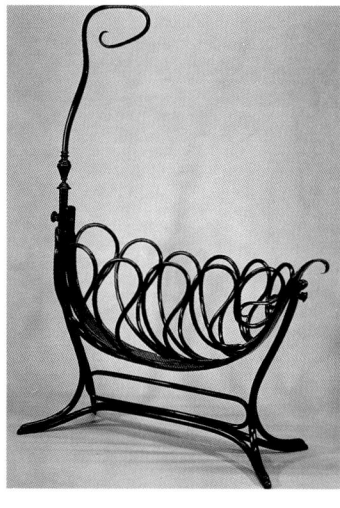

19 / CRADLE, MODEL NO. 1573

Manufacturer: Jacob & Josef Kohn, after 1904

Beech

81½ x 25¾ x 55 in.

20 / TABLE, MODEL NO. 902

Manufacturer: Jacob & Josef Kohn, after 1904

Beech

27¾ x 45 x 32 in.

Collection of Shelby Williams Industries, Inc.

21 / TOILET STAND, MODEL NO. 2

Manufacturer: Gebrüder Thonet, after 1884

Beech, mirror glass

61½ x 29¾ x 18 in.

22 / WASHING STAND, MODEL NO. 973

Manufacturer: Jacob & Josef Kohn, after 1890s

Beech, mirror glass

62½ x 34 x 25 in.

23 / WASHING STAND [ALTERED SUPERSTRUCTURE]

Manufacturer: Gebrüder Thonet, after 1895

Beech, leather (replacement)

36 x 36 x 19 in.

24 / CARD TABLE, MODEL NO. 3

Manufacturer: Gebrüder Thonet, after 1895

Beech, felt (replacement)

30¾ x 38¾ x 19½ in.

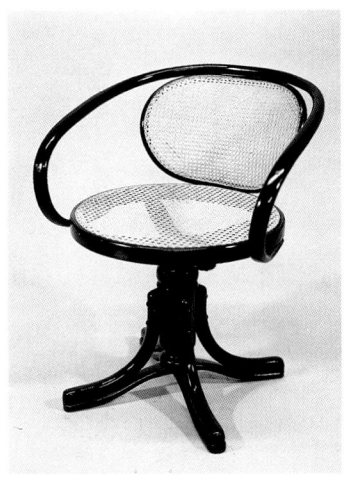

25 / REVOLVING ARMCHAIR, MODEL NO. 1

Manufacturer: Gebrüder Thonet, after 1895
Beech, cane, metal
29¾ x 23 x 23 in.
Collection of Shelby Williams Industries, Inc.

26 / SIDE CHAIR, MODEL NO. 66

Manufacturer: Gebrüder Thonet, after 1895
Beech, wood laminate
34⅛ x 15¾ x 17½ in.

27 / SIDE CHAIR, MODEL NO. 124

Manufacturer: Gebrüder Thonet, after 1904
Beech, wood laminate
34½ x 14¾ x 16¾ in.

28 / SIDE CHAIR, MODEL NO. 120

Manufacturer: Gebrüder Thonet, after 1904
Beech, wood laminate
35½ x 16⅛ x 19¾ in.

29 / SIDE CHAIR, MODEL NO. 100

Manufacturer: Gebrüder Thonet, after 1904
Beech, wood laminate
34 x 15 x 17¾ in.

30 / SIDE CHAIR, MODEL NO. 220

Manufacturer: Jacob & Josef Kohn, after 1904
Beech, wood laminate
34½ x 15 x 19 in.

31 / SIDE CHAIR, MODEL NO. 70 (ONE OF A PAIR)

Manufacturer: Jacob & Josef Kohn, after 1906
Beech, wood laminate
38 x 15¾ x 19¾ in.

32 / ARMCHAIR, MODEL NO. 3

Manufacturer: Gebrüder Thonet, after 1904
Beech, wood laminate
31¾ x 23⅜ x 22⅛ in.

33 / STOOL, MODEL NO. 4703

Manufacturer: D. G. Fischel Söhne (1870-1938)
Beech, wood laminate
19 x 14¼ in.

34 / "FIRESIDE" ARMCHAIR, MODEL NO. 3

Manufacturer: Gebrüder Thonet, after 1905
Beech, cane
45½ x 22¾ x 20¼ in

35 / SIDE CHAIR, MODEL NO. 55

Manufacturer: Jacob & Josef Kohn, after 1904
Beech, cane
33¼ x 16⅝ x 18⅝ in.
Collection of Shelby Williams Industries, Inc.

36 / SIDE CHAIR, MODEL NO. 248A

Manufacturer: Jacob & Josef Kohn, after 1906
Beech, wood laminate
35 x 16 x 19¾ in.

37 / PORTABLE ARMCHAIR FOR INVALIDS, MODEL NO. 6991

Manufacturer: Gebrüder Thonet, after 1904
Beech, cane, metal
37⁹⁄₁₆ x 23½ x 54½ in.

38 / SETTEE, MODEL NO. 715/C

Designer: Gustav Siegel, c. 1900
Manufacturer: Jacob & Josef Kohn, after 1900
Beech, metal, upholstery (reproduction)
30 x 48 x 22½ in.

39 / ARMCHAIR, MODEL NO. 715

Designer: Gustav Siegel, c. 1900
Manufacturer: Jacob & Josef Kohn, after 1900
Beech, metal, upholstery (reproduction)
30 x 21½ x 21½ in.

40 / SETTEE, MODEL NO. 412/C

Designer: Gustav Siegel, c. 1902
Manufacturer: Jacob & Josef Kohn, after 1902
Beech, brass, upholstery (reproduction)
32¾ x 47 x 24 in.

41 / SIDE CHAIR, MODEL NO. 412 (ONE OF FOUR)
Designer: Gustav Siegel, c. 1902
Manufacturer: Jacob & Josef Kohn, after 1902
Beech, brass, upholstery (reproduction)
33 x 16¼ x 18 in.

42 / BENCH, MODEL NO.412/S
Designer: Gustav Siegel, c. 1902
Manufacturer: Jacob & Josef Kohn, after 1902
Beech, brass, upholstery (reproduction)
25¼ x 22¾ x 13¾ in.

43 / SIDE CHAIR, MODEL NO. 330
Designer: Josef Hoffmann, c. 1901
Manufacturer: Jacob & Josef Kohn, after 1901
Beech, wood laminate, brass, upholstery (reproduction)
37½ x 18⅞ x 19¼ in.

44 / ARMCHAIR, MODEL NO.719/F
Manufacturer: Jacob & Josef Kohn, designed before 1906
Beech, brass, upholstery (replacement)
34 x 22 x 22½ in.

45 / ARMCHAIR, MODEL NO. 6585
Manufacturer: Gebrüder Thonet, after 1907
Beech, upholstery (replacement)
35 x 26½ x 22½ in.

46 / SIDE CHAIR, MODEL NO.725/B
Manufacturer: Jacob & Josef Kohn, after 1906
Beech, upholstery (replacement)
34½ x 16¾ x 20¾ in.

47 / TOILET TABLE
Manufacturer: Gebrüder Thonet, after 1906
Beech, wood laminate, mirror glass
53³⁄₁₆ x 23¼ x 18½ in.

48 / CLOAK STAND, MODEL NO. 5
Manufacturer: Gebrüder Thonet, after 1904
Beech, wood laminate
72⅞ x 35⅜ in.

49 / ARMCHAIR, MODEL NO. 511

Manufacturer: Gebrüder Thonet, after 1905
Beech, wood laminate
38¾ x 21¼ x 25¼ in.

50 / SIDE CHAIR, MODEL NO. 440

Manufacturer: Gebrüder Thonet, after 1904
Beech, upholstery
35⅝ x 16½ x 19¼ in.

51 / SIDE CHAIR, MODEL NO. 301A

Manufacturer: Gebrüder Thonet, after 1906
Beech, upholstery (replacement)
35½ x 16½ x 18¼ in.

52 / SIDE CHAIR

Manufacturer: Gebrüder Thonet, probably c.1905/1910
Beech, wood laminate, metal
36 x 18³⁄₁₆ x 17½ in.

53 / STOOL

Manufacturer: possibly Gebrüder Thonet, c.1905/1910
Beech, wood laminate
21¾ x 14¼ in.

54 / SIDE CHAIR

Manufacturer: Gebrüder Thonet, c. 1920
Beech, cane
36⅛ x 16½ x 19⁹⁄₁₆ in.

55 / ARMCHAIR, MODEL NO. A967

Manufacturer: Gebrüder Thonet, c. 1925
Beech, wood laminate
31 x 21½ x 20¾ in.

56 / SIDE CHAIR, MODEL NO. 96/5

Designer: attributed to Josef Urban, c. 1921
Manufacturer: Gebrüder Thonet
Beech, upholstery (replacement)
36⅛ x 17½ x 21 in.

57 / SIDE CHAIR, MODEL NO. 169

Manufacturer: D. G. Fischel Söhne (1870–1938)
Beech, upholstery
36 x 14¾ x 18½ in.

58 / SWIVEL CHAIR

Manufacturer: Gebrüder Thonet, c. 1920s
Beech, wood laminate, metal
34¼ x 20½ x 20¾ in.

59 / SWIVEL STOOL

Manufacturer: Gebrüder Thonet, c. 1920s
Beech, wood laminate, metal
31½ x 16½ x 16½ in.

60 / ARMCHAIR

Manufacturer: R. L. Seymour (American), c. 1920/1925
Beech, cane
39 x 21⅜ x 23¾ in.

61 / SIDE CHAIR, VARIATION ON MODEL NO. B5

Designer: Marcel Breuer (American, b. Hungary, 1902–1981), 1925/1926
Manufacturer: Gebrüder Thonet, after 1928
Tubular steel, fabric
34¼ x 18⅜ x 21½ in.

62 / ARMCHAIR, MODEL NO. B11

Designer: Marcel Breuer (American, b. Hungary, 1902–1981), 1926/1927
Manufacturer: Gebrüder Thonet, after 1928
Tubular steel, fabric
34 x 20⅛ x 20½ in.

63 / TABLE, MODEL NO. B27

Designer: Marcel Breuer (American, b. Hungary, 1902–1981), 1928
Manufacturer: Gebrüder Thonet, from 1928
Tubular steel, glass, rubber
23 x 27½ in.

64 / UMBRELLA STAND, MODEL NO. B38

Manufacturer: Gebrüder Thonet, from c. 1929
Tubular steel, metal
20 x 15 in.

65 / DESK, MODEL NO. B91

Designer: Marcel Breuer (American, b. Hungary, 1902–1981), c. 1930
Manufacturer: Gebrüder Thonet, from c. 1935
Tubular steel, wood
27 1/8 x 35 3/4 x 19 1/4 in.

66 / ARMCHAIR, MODEL NO. B261

Designer: Emile Guillot (French), c. 1929
Manufacturer: Thonet Frères (France), c. 1929
Tubular steel, wood
33 x 20 1/4 x 21 3/4 in.

67 / ARMCHAIR

Designer: Gilbert Rhode (American, 1894–1944), 1929
Manufacturer: Heywood-Wakefield Furniture Company (Wakefield, Mass.), from 1929
Wood, upholstery (replacement)
32 1/2 x 22 1/2 x 23 1/2 in.

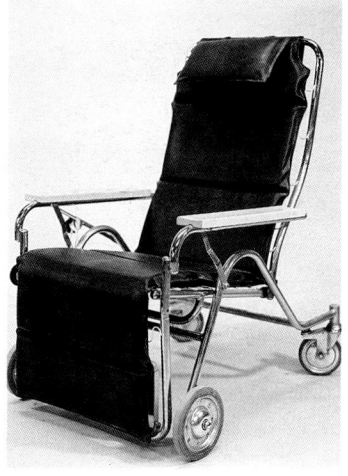

68 / WHEEL CHAIR ("SIESTA CHAIR")

Designers: Hans Luckhardt (German, 1890–1954) and Wassili Luckhardt (German, 1888–1972), c. 1940
Manufacturer: Gebrüder Thonet (Frankenberg), after 1940
Tubular steel, wood, rubber, upholstery
45 x 28 3/4 x 37 in.
Collection of Shelby Williams Industries, Inc.

69 / SIDE CHAIR, MODEL NO. 1250-B1

Designed: 1945
Manufacturer: Thonet Industries, Inc. (USA), c. 1950
Plywood, plastic
31 1/2 x 15 3/4 x 20 1/2 in.

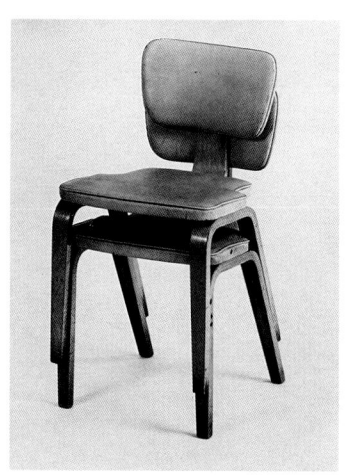

70 / STACKING CHAIRS, MODEL NO. 1311

Designer: Bruno Weill (American, b. Austria, 1893–1962), c. 1951
Manufacturer: Thonet Industries, Inc. (USA)
Plywood, vinyl
30 x 17 x 18 3/4 in.

71 / SIDE CHAIR, MODEL NO. 1312

Designed: c. 1950
Manufacturer: Thonet Industries, Inc. (USA)
Plywood, vinyl
30 1/2 x 18 1/4 x 23 in.

72 / SIDE CHAIR, MODEL NO. 1177

Designer: Bruno Weill (American, b. Austria, 1893–1962), c. 1955
Manufacturer: Thonet Industries, Inc. (USA)
Plywood, vinyl
32 3/4 x 17 x 20 in.

73 / ARMCHAIR, MODEL NO. 3001

Designer: Bruno Weill (American, b. Austria, 1893–1962), c. 1945
Manufacturer: Thonet Industries, Inc. (USA)
Plywood, vinyl
31½ x 22 x 20½ in.

74 / "SOF-TECH" SIDE CHAIR, MODEL NO. 200C

Designer: David Rowland (American), 1979
Manufacturer: Thonet Industries, Inc. (USA)
Tubular steel, Soflex (vinyl-coated plastic)
29¾ x 19½ x 19 in.

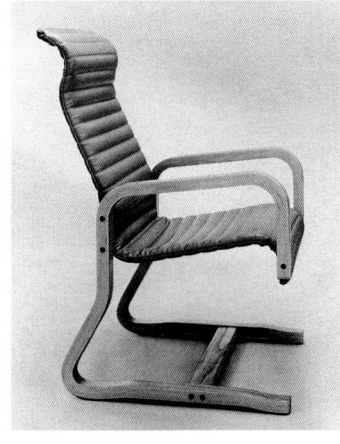

75 / ARMCHAIR ("KANGAROO" CHAIR), MODEL NO. 1390

Designers: Joe Russo (American, b. 1930) and Rick Sonder (American, b. 1929), c. 1975
Manufacturer: Thonet Industries, Inc. (USA)
Oak, plywood, vinyl
42 x 23⅝ x 21½ in.

76 / ARMCHAIR, MODEL NO. 1318

Designer: Peter Danko (American, b. 1949), 1980
Manufacturer: Thonet Industries, Inc. (USA)
Plywood, upholstery
30¾ x 22 x 24 in.
Collection of Shelby Williams Industries, Inc.

77 / SIDE CHAIR, MODEL NO. 1318

Designer: Peter Danko (American, b. 1949), 1980
Manufacturer: Thonet Industries, Inc. (USA)
Plywood, upholstery
31 x 22 x 23 in.
Collection of Shelby Williams Industries, Inc.

78 / "PETITT PLY" ARMCHAIR, MODEL NO. 1322

Designer: Don Petitt (American, b. 1925), 1981
Manufacturer: Thonet Industries, Inc. (USA)
Plywood, upholstery
33 x 24¼ x 26 in.

79 / STACKING CHAIRS ("ATTIVA" CHAIR), MODEL NO. 5000

Designer: Jerome Caruso (American, b. 1937), 1989
Manufacturer: Thonet Industries, Inc. (USA), since 1990
Plastic, metal
31 x 21¾ x 22 in.

CATALOG SOURCES

The Art Journal Illustrated Catalogue: The Industry of All Nations (London, 1851).

Asenbaum, Stefan and Julius Hummel, eds. *Gebogenes Holz: Konstruktive Entwürfe Wien 1840–1910* exh. cat. Kunstlerhaus Wien (Vienna, 1979).

Austria at the International Exhibition of 1862 (Vienna, 1862).

Bang, Ole. "Thonet and England," *The Journal of The Decorative Arts Society, 1850 to the Present*, no. 11 (1987), pp. 27–31.

Benton, Tim, Charlotte Benton, and Dennis Sharp, eds. *Architecture and Design: 1890–1939* (New York, 1975).

Brandstätter, Christian. *Das Wiener Kaffeehaus* (Vienna, 1978).

Breckner, Gunter. *Josef Hoffmann Sanatorium Purkersdorf*, exh. cat. Galerie Metropol (New York and Vienna, n.d.).

Candilis, G., A. Blomstedt, T. Frangoulis, and M. I. Amorin. *Bugholzmöbel,* 2nd ed. (Stuttgart, 1984).

Deutsch, Davida. "Samuel Gragg's Boston Bentwood Chairs, 1809," *Antiques Magazine* 107–108 (May 1975), p. 939.

Droste, Magdalena, and Manfred Ludewig. *Marcel Breuer Design* (Berlin, 1992).

Dry, Graham, ed. *Thonet Brothers: 1888 Catalogue,* repr. (Munich, 1979).

———, ed. *Jacob & Josef Kohn Bugholzmöbel Der Katalog von 1916,* 3rd repr. ed. (Munich, 1985).

"First Austrian Bentwood Furniture Manufacturing Company (Limited) Jacob and Josef Kohn," in *Historisch-biographische Blätter (Industrie, Handel und Gewerbe)* (Berlin and Vienna, 1902).

Gebhard, David. *Josef Hoffmann: Design Classics,* exh. cat. Fort Worth [Tex.] Art Museum (1983).

Gebrüder Thonet. *Thonet Stahlrohrmöbel,* sales cat. (Frankenberg, Germany, 1935).

———. *Verkaufskatalog 1895,* repr. (Frankenberg, Germany, 1980).

Gere, Charlotte. *Nineteenth-Century Decoration: The Art of the Interior* (London, 1989).

Hanks, David A. *Innovative Furniture in America from 1800 to the Present* (New York, 1981).

Himmelheber, Georg. *Biedermeier Furniture,* trans. and ed. by Simon Jervis (London, 1974).

Holme, Charles, ed. *The Art Revival in Austria* (London, 1906).

Jacob & Josef Kohn. [Sales cat.] (Vienna, [c. 1881]).

Jervis, Simon. *Art and Design in Europe* (London, 1987).

———. *Furniture of about 1900 from Austria and Hungary in the Victoria & Albert Museum* (London, 1985).

Kallir, Jane. *Viennese Design and the Wiener Werkstätte,* exh. cat. Galerie St. Etienne (New York, 1986).

Kane, Patricia E. "Samuel Gragg: His Bentwood Fancy Chairs," *Yale University Art Gallery Bulletin* 33, no. 2 (1971), pp. 26–37.

Lang, Helmut W. "Auch im Kampf gegen die Konkurrenz. Thonets Motto: Biegen oder Brechen," *Das Wilde Biedermeier 1800–1848 Parnass Sonderheft* 4 (1987), pp. 56–67.

Levetus, A. S. "Austrian Architecture and Decoration," *The Studio Year-Book of Decorative Art* (London, 1908), pp. xlv–xlvi and plates.

———. "Austrian Architecture and Decoration," *The Studio Year-Book of Decorative Art* (London, 1911), pp. 213–62.

Loos, Adolf. *Spoken into the Void: Collected Essays 1897–1900* (Cambridge, Mass., 1982).

Mang, Karl. *Thonet Bugholzmöbel* (Vienna, 1982).

Massobrio, Giovanna, and Paolo Portoghesi. *Casa Thonet* (Rome-Bari, 1980).

Meyer, Christian. *Josef Hoffmann: Architect and Designer, 1870–1956,* exh. cat. Galerie Metropol (Vienna and New York, [1981]).

Noever, Peter, ed. *Josef Hoffmann Designs,* exh. cat. MAK-Austrian Museum of Applied Arts (Vienna, 1992).

Ostergard, Derek E., ed. *Bent Wood and Metal Furniture: 1850–1946* (New York, 1987).

Ottillinger, Eva B. "August Kitschelt's Metal Furniture Factory and Viennese Metal Furniture in the Nineteenth Century," *Furniture History* XXV (1989), pp. 235–49.

———. "The 'Kaiser Salon' and the Beginnings of the Rococo Revival in Vienna," *Furniture History* XXVII (1991), pp. 137–48.

Schaefer, Herwin. *Nineteenth-Century Modern: The Functional Tradition in Victorian Design* (New York, 1970).

Schorske, Carl E. *Fin-de-Siècle Vienna: Politics and Culture* (New York, 1980).

Seckler, Eduard F. *Josef Hoffmann: The Architectural Work. Monograph and Catalogue of Works* (Princeton, N.J., 1985).

Simpson, Lisa. *Thonet Furniture, 1830–1990,* exh. brochure Knoxville [Tenn.] Museum of Art (1990).

Sitz-Gelegenheiten: Bugholz- und Stahlrohrmöbel von Thonet, exh. cat. Germanisches Nationalmuseum (Nürnberg, 1989).

Simoníková, Jaromíra. *D. G. Fischel Sons: The 1915 Catalogue* (Munich, 1992).

Thonet Bentwood & Other Furniture: The 1904 Illustrated Catalogue, repr., intro. by Christopher Wilk (New York, 1980).

Thonet Brothers. [Sales cat. for North America] (Vienna, c. 1881).

Thonet, George. Letter to Manfred Steinfeld, Sept. 6, 1989.

Thonet Industries, Inc. *Furniture Designs,* cat. no. 5111 (New York, n.d.).

Vegesack, Alexander von. *Deutsche Stahlrohrmöbel: 650 Modelle aus Katalogen von 1927–1958* (Munich, 1986).

———. *Michael Thonet Leben und Werk* (Munich, 1987).

———. *Das Thonet Buch* (Munich, 1987).

Vegesack, Alexander von, Marie-Claire Mayer, and Marc Bascou. *L'industrie Thonet,* exh. cat. Musee d'Orsay (Paris, 1986).

Vienna in the Age of Schubert: The Biedermeier Interior, 1815–1848, exh. cat. Victoria and Albert Museum, London (1979).

Waissenberger, Robert. *Vienna in the Biedermeier Era, 1815–1848* (New York, 1986).

Wilk, Christopher. *Thonet: 150 Years of Furniture* (Woodbury, N.Y., 1980).